BIG BET LEADERSHIP

Your Transformation Playbook
for Winning in the Hyper-Digital Era

JOHN ROSSMAN
and KEVIN MCCAFFREY

RODIN
BOOKS™

BIG BET LEADERSHIP

"*Big Bet Leadership* outlines a groundbreaking guide for enterprises navigating the treacherous path of transformation and innovation. Packed with actionable strategies, this compelling book redefines the playbook for senior management, urging leaders to rethink their methods, foster a dynamic environment and take the reins of change."

—**Mike Steep, founder, Disruptive Technology & Digital Cities Program, Stanford University; former SVP Xerox PARC**

"This playbook is destined to be a cult classic for business leaders and their advisors to change the trajectory and future of their business, their culture and their leadership techniques. Don't proceed with your transformation without Big Bet Leadership."

—**Joel Bines, board member & advisor, retired AlixPartners Managing Director, author of *The Metail Economy***

"Ninety percent of the world knows they need to change. Only 10% are ready to change. *Big Bet Leadership* is for that 10%."

—**Dr. Mark Goulston, author of *Just Listen* and *Talking to Crazy*; UCLA professor of psychiatry, former FBI and police hostage negotiation trainer**

"The overwhelming majority of business executives get paid to make small bets. This book is not for them. This book is for the few who make the big bets required to build the legendary companies, products, and categories of the future."

—**Christopher Lochhead, bestselling author of *Play Bigger & 22 Laws of Category Design***

"John Rossman has taken his experience from the early days at Amazon and helped apply those principals to help companies operate more effectively. His new book *Big Bet Leadership* simplifies the connections between innovation, value propositions and customer pain points. It provides frameworks to help marketers play a more strategic role in companies by maximizing impact while simultaneously reducing risk. Worth your time!"

—Ed Nevraumont, senior advisor,
Warburg Pincus

"Absolutely wonderful! The authors walk the reader through leading change with simple, but profound principles that pay big dividends."

—(Ret) 4 Star General Gustave Perna

"*Big Bet Leadership* is a game changer for leaders looking to drive transformation and deliver remarkable results. Rossman's wealth of experience, combined with his practical insights, and engaging storytelling, make this book a must-read guide for anyone seeking to lead with vision, embrace risk, and create a lasting impact. *Big Bet Leadership* is a roadmap for deeply understanding, in fact obsessing, about customers and thinking in outcomes. Prepare to be inspired, challenged, and equipped with the tools to lead with purpose and deliver tangible outcomes."

—Gary Michel, former Chair and CEO
JELD-WEN, Inc., *Forbes* Featured Author,
Keynote Speaker, Director, and Advisor

First Edition

Hardcover ISBN 978-1-957588-22-3
eBook ISBN 978-1-957588-23-0

PUBLISHED BY RODIN BOOKS INC.
666 Old Country Road
Suite 510
Garden City, New York 11530

www.rodinbooks.com

Book and cover design by Alexia Garaventa

Manufactured in the United States of America

RODIN
BOOKS™

BIG BET
LEADERSHIP

Your Transformation Playbook

for Winning in the Hyper-Digital Era

CONTENTS

PREFACE
WHY WRITE THIS BOOK?

There are countless books that make the case for digital transformation, innovation, and business model reinvention; others that deal with Agile frameworks and innovation programs and styles; and bountiful stories about the companies and leaders of both the disruptors and the disrupted. Those works are important, but they are not sufficient.

Big Bet Leadership is oriented at a different altitude and for a complementary purpose. This playbook highlights the key failure points of transformations, innovation programs, major technology initiatives and other high-risk strategies, defines a guiding policy or approach to address the point of failure, and describes steps and tactics to gain the desired outcome. These approaches are at an actionable level for executive implementation.

The mission of *Big Bet Leadership* is to aid leaders in doing a central part of their job, which is in leading transformations.

That is why we wrote this book. But why now?

We are writing *Big Bet Leadership* now because the job of leading transformations is simultaneously getting harder while the need for them has never been greater. Our belief is that leading successful transformations and innovation must become a leadership core competency, which it is not today for most leaders and companies.

MEGA FORCES SHAPING AMERICA'S NEED TO INNOVATE

There are three mega forces shaping America's need and opportunity to drive productivity and innovation.

The first mega force is disruptive technologies such as generative AI and quantum computing. There are many types of artificial intelligence and machine learning, and many other disruptive technologies. Computer vision, the Internet of Things (IoT), cloud and edge computing, augmented and virtual reality, and 5G technology are just some of the game-changing technologies. More are on the horizon, with fusion energy a potentially complete game changer.

Why are these disruptive technologies game-changing? Because customer value propositions as well as company organizational structures, operating models, and cost structures can be radically reinvented by using what is often a combination of these disruptive technologies.

The second mega force is the aging of America's workforce. In 1995, approximately 88 percent of the US population was under the age of 65. Today, it is 82 percent. In 1995, the US birthrate was approximately 15 per 1,000 people. Today, it is approximately 11. In 1995, approximately 3 percent of the US labor force was over 65. Currently, it is approximately 6 percent. By 2050, it is projected to more than double to over 13 percent.

Our available workforce is aging, and that is a challenge confronting most of the world's major economies. This mega force will drive substantial but hard-to-predict disruptions to companies' organizational structures, operating models, and cost structures.

The third mega force is the growth of spending on entitlement programs such as Social Security and Medicare as well as the cost of serving the US debt. The Congressional Budget Office forecasts US government spending on entitlement programs plus net interest on US debt to grow from 56% of total federal spending in 2023 to 74% by 2050.[1] Growth in spending on entitlement programs and debt payments will create upward pressure on taxes and downward pressure on spending on infrastructure, education, defense, and other discretionary spending programs.

One effective way to reduce the burden of the debt and entitlements obligation is to improve productivity, increasing the size of the economy. The aging of the workforce will create macroeconomic conditions encouraging companies to realize dramatic versus incremental increases in productivity. Disruptive technologies provide the essential enabler for the innovation and retooling.

This tumultuous backdrop, formed by the combination of these three mega forces, will be further stoked by the monetary war chests that private equity, venture capital, and Big Tech companies are poised to invest in fueling an ever-accelerating rate of disruption. Global private capital raises totaled $1.3 trillion in 2022, up from $448 billion in 2012.[2] Over the same decade, US venture capital assets under management grew from $255 billion to $1.2 trillion.[3] The combined annual operating free cash flow of Amazon, Apple, Facebook, Google, and Microsoft grew nearly fourfold, from approximately $100 billion in 2012 to nearly $400 billion per year in 2022.[4] Combined, these trillion-dollar war chests will fund the creation of dramatically more efficient operating models and cost structures and the technology to fuel this battle of innovation and efficiency.

These mega forces will feed into each other like a vortex, building an overriding theme for business and society—that of a chaotic environment of dramatic change with successful business operators realizing productivity and cost model advantages that separate them from their competition.

THE STARTING POINT

Netscape went public on August 9, 1995, and that date is often used as a historical marker for the start of the current digital era. ChatGPT was released on November 30, 2022. We believe that in the coming years the release date of ChatGPT will be another historical marker for a new era of competition: the Hyper-Digital Era.

This will be an era with more dramatic business winners and losers. The winners will include categories and companies unknown to us today. The losers will include organizations and brands that today appear to be under no threat, perhaps even the big winners of the first digital era.

Those companies and leaders who lack daring, clarity, and velocity will typically find themselves on the wrong side of history. We write this book to assist those who are the opposite—ready to act with daring, clarity, and velocity to compete for the future.

YOUR GUIDES

John Rossman and Kevin McCaffrey are your guides and form the perfect team to help advance your leadership to win in the Hyper-Digital Era.

John is a thirty-five-year veteran of leading complex change, technology, and business innovation initiatives. He started his career at Accenture in an advanced technology team that was building object-oriented and early graphical user interface applications on Unix workstations. He was a partner at Arthur Andersen and then an executive at a technology startup, which was a victim of the dot-com bubble.

He served in key leadership roles in the early days of Amazon. com, when the survival of the company was doubted. While the media and industry experts referred to Amazon as "Amazon.toast," "Amazon.con," and "Amazon.org," the latter being a jab at the potential—or lack thereof—for profitability, Amazon transitioned from the world's biggest bookstore to the everything store and a platform business model. John was the Director of Merchant Integration and played a key leadership role in launching the Marketplace business in 2002, which was called a "dreamy business" by Bezos.[5]

John embraced his knowledge and experience and brought it to a worldwide audience as the author of three books about competing in the digital era: *The Amazon Way: The Leadership Principles Behind the World's Most Disruptive Company*; *Think Like Amazon: 50 1/2 Ideas to Become a Digital Leader*; and *The Amazon Way on IoT*.

Since leaving Amazon.com, John has applied and adapted the leadership, strategy, and mechanisms of Amazon for use at dozens of clients, including serving as Innovation Advisor to T-Mobile and Senior Technology Advisor to the Bill and Melinda Gates Foundation. He has presented hundreds of keynotes on leadership, innovation, and digital transformation. He was a Managing Director at Alvarez and Marsal for twelve years before founding Rossman Partners in order to assist his clients on leadership, strategy, and complex problem solving, typically related to a digital strategy or operating model transformation. He is a senior advisor to several companies including Wilson Perumal, a management consulting organization, and with GrokIt Technologies, an autonomous AI workforce and protocol company.

Kevin spent five years in the belly of the beast at T-Mobile learning from the best about how to place Big Bets effectively and supporting T-Mobile's executive team in designing strategy and operations capable of furthering the Un-carrier legacy. He led innovation efforts at T-Mobile, where he first formed a working partnership with John. After T-Mobile, Kevin was hired as the Director of Operations within the Strategy and Operations team at Google Ads, where he led initiatives to better adapt the Google Ads operating model for sustaining the long-term growth of one of the most successful business models in modern history. His work is framed by his experience supporting dozens of Fortune 500 executives in navigating their companies' transformations as a consultant with McKinsey & Company. He is now a research and development partner to Rossman Partners.

INTRODUCTION

"Ironically, in a changing world, playing it safe is one of the riskiest things you can do."

—REID HOFFMAN

In 2013, at the annual Consumer Electronics Show in Las Vegas, T-Mobile CEO John Legere confidently stepped onto the stage, prepared to place a bet. But this was no ordinary Vegas gamble. It was a high-stakes wager gambling the future of his company—this was a *Big Bet*.

With a captivating blend of humor and audacity, Legere declared war on his competitors and the mobile industry's tarnished reputation. His rallying cry signaled a radical new strategy: No Contracts. No Data Plan. No Overages. "We are the Un-carrier!" The impact was electric, igniting the audience, stirring the media, and inspiring his team back in Bellevue.

While Legere is often celebrated for his bold leadership, keen insights, and strategic acumen, his true genius lies in understanding what all leaders must do: assess their situation, recognize their strengths and limitations, and make a Big Bet when it counts.

But Legere didn't stop there. He constructed a powerful engine capable of churning out one Big Bet after another, dubbing them "Un-carrier Moves." Over several years, T-Mobile executed twelve Un-carrier Moves, driving more than twenty consecutive quarters of industry-leading subscriber growth, record-breaking net promoter scores, and an enterprise valuation that grew over 700 percent.

Legere was a master of *Big Bet Leadership*, defining and harnessing the systematic transformation of T-Mobile from a financially hamstrung, laggard, fourth-position mobile telecommunications provider to a market-leading brand viewed as the market innovator.

Legere's Big Bet challenged the industry orthodoxy of fixed contracts, roaming fees, and data caps, but Big Bets can take many other forms. Legere's Big Bet is just one type. Let's identify the other common types of Big Bets this playbook is for:

First, there are go-to-market and brand re-positioning initiatives. These are a fundamental repositioning of a product or service within the marketplace, such as the T-Mobile Un-carrier announcement.

Second, there are digital transformations. A digital transformation is the integration of digital technology into all aspects of a business, fundamentally reshaping how it operates and delivers value to customers, with a focus on improving efficiency, innovation, and the customer experience.

Third, there are innovation programs, which are a systematic approach to incubating transformative new businesses and product line extensions. When a concept from the innovation program involves a significant change or investment, it is a Big Bet.

Fourth, there are technology platform investments. Often there is a thin veneer of a business change and justification, but at their core these are 80 percent major system overhauls, upgrades, and transitions.

Fifth, there are operating model transitions. An operating model is a framework outlining how an organization aligns its resources, processes, and technologies to deliver its value proposition to customers effectively and to achieve its strategic objectives. When the operating model involves a significant change or investment, it is a Big Bet.

Sixth, there are mergers and acquisitions. Both pre-deal diligence and post-transaction merger-integration programs are typically Big Bets because there is a clear thesis for benefit.

All of these Big Bets are connected by these realities: they almost always underdeliver in benefits, take longer and cost more than planned, and oftentimes are considered failures.

WHY BIG BETS FAIL

An examination of the data suggests that the likelihood of John Legere successfully executing even one Big Bet was slim, let alone a series of them in rapid succession. Digital transformations, operational shifts, product launches, innovation initiatives, large-scale technology migrations, mergers, and other Big Bets suffer a staggering failure rate of over 70 percent. Every piece of research we've examined converges on a similar finding—substantial and critical transformations are typically considered failures:

- "An alarming 73% of enterprises failed to derive any business value from their digital transformation, and 78% fell short of meeting their business objectives."[1]

- "89% of companies have launched a flavor of digital transformation. But they only captured 31% of the expected revenue lift and realized just 25% of total cost savings."[2]

- "According to most studies, between 70 and 90 percent of acquisitions fail."[3]

- A study of 1,471 IT projects revealed that while the average cost overrun was 27%, an alarming one in six projects experienced overruns of 200% and were delayed by 70%.[4]

The true hazards of such major initiatives stem not just from the high likelihood of underperformance or budgetary excesses, but from the genuine risk of colossal failure. One global expert on megaprojects, Bent Flyvbjerg, notes that "In total, only 8.5 percent of projects hit the mark on both cost and time. And a minuscule 0.5 percent nail cost, time and benefits."[5]

Is there hope?

Our responsibility is to learn from both legends and failures, proactively sidestepping the many pitfalls, enabling our organizations to confidently pursue innovations, technology initiatives, digital transformations, and operational adaptations that drive exceptional financial results and a formidable competitive edge.

John Legere isn't alone. There are a few leaders who have proven an ability to systematically beat the dismal odds of getting Big Bets right. Leaders like Jeff Bezos, Elon Musk, and Satya Nadella repeatedly succeed at Big Bets and then can take on more of them, while other leaders roll the dice and fail more often than not. Studying the leadership styles of these Big Bet legends offers lessons and makes it clear that they act in ways that Big Bet losers do not.

Imagine possessing a leadership playbook akin to a mystical codex, filled with insights empowering the holder to conquer complex problems, challenges, and transformations and avoid the traps and enemies hidden on the path to treasure. If you could have a map illuminating your path, steering you through perilous journeys and pushing you up to the limits of your company's potential, teaching you how to compete and win in the next era of competition and hyper-digital companies, would you pay attention? Would you be willing to reconsider the dogma of traditional management practices?

SOLVING WICKED PROBLEMS

The CEO of a company has a unique perspective and obligation. Their viewpoint is based on seeing the world and their business through the lens of risk. The CEO job is to always scan for the enterprise risks that might threaten the organization—competitive, capability, capital, cyber, reputation, regulatory, and legal. More than ever, there is the existential risk that disruptive technologies and artificial intelligence represent to products, services, operations, and business models. Responding to these risks and complex problems is what drives the response—the strategy, the transformation, the initiatives.

Risks are often both threats and opportunities. Big Bets don't stem from simple or predictable problems and challenges. Big Bets are a response to multi-sided, complex, and difficult-to-predict problems with many facets to them. These are often referred to as wicked problems.

A wicked problem is a complex situation that is difficult to define, unique, has multiple constraints, has no universally agreed-upon solution, and is one in which solutions are difficult to test. Wicked problems can happen at any level of the enterprise, from an all-encompassing situation, such as a business turnaround or digital transformation, or at a functional or department level, such as a legacy core technology platform transition or a supply chain transformation.

In his seminal book *Good Strategy/Bad Strategy: The Difference and Why it Matters*,[6] Richard Rumelt argues that a good strategy is a coherent set of actions designed to address a challenge or a specific complex problem, while a bad strategy is an ambiguous or incoherent plan either not attached to a specific challenge or one that fails to confront or resolve the crux of a problem. Good strategy is marked by a kernel consisting of three elements: a diagnosis, a guiding policy, and a set of coherent actions.

Big Bet Leadership builds off Rumelt's work, giving a structured collection of guidelines, strategies, and tactics that will assist organizations and executives in achieving specific goals and solving wicked problems. This playbook provides a structured and paced approach to problem-solving and decision-making, outlining innovative practices, key principles, and practical steps. The playbook includes identifying the core issue or challenge, a generalized principle in approaching and solving the challenge, and tactics to demonstrate a path to action. This guide develops not just good strategy for wicked problems, validating the riskiest parts of the strategy from the inception and setting up the effective transition to strategy execution, but addresses the most significant risks and challenges in executing this strategy.

It is when attempting to solve these difficult challenges, in these calculated moments in which a path is chosen, where management either prove their mettle or set out upon another foolish journey. In all cases, Big Bets have material risk. And in most cases, they fail. Yet these are the Big Bets we must make. **The mission of Big Bet Leadership is to help you mitigate the risks while maintaining the ambitious goals that motivate us to transform.**

PLAYING IT SAFE

Instead of pretending Big Bets are not needed or accepting high failure rates with marginal improvements, *Big Bet Leadership* enables a dramatic reduction of the failure risk while simultaneously increasing the size of the prize. By raising the success rate of Big Bets, we enable a more aggressive mindset and posture. This is how you will compete and win in the Hyper-Digital Era.

The choice in front of management is ultimately one of four:

Do we avoid and resist the need for digital transformations, systematic innovation, and operating model advancements, thus avoiding the poker table of Big Bets?

Do we accept the low odds of success that current management best practices deliver, thus accepting a rigged game with a high probability of failure?

Do we deny ourselves intellectual honesty, believing that our strategic plans can predict the future and our agile project management makes us different?

Or . . .

Do we intentionally choose to become a shark, the commanding player at the poker table of Big Bets? This is a playbook for leaders who deliberately choose to become a shark and a Big Bet legend. They want to win.

Leaders are under constant pressure to produce improved earnings, growth, and new lines of business and revenue. Simultaneously, they need to improve productivity and efficiency, lower cost structures, and get more done with less.

Leaders who can't stomach the inherent gambling involved in addressing those topics are likely not playing to win. Companies that fail to navigate them successfully are overtaken by rivals. This is why disruption, declining profitability, commoditization, irrelevancy, and eventual company demise happen.

Big Bets are not optional unless you are in a protected environment. The business world is divided into those leaders who do this well and those who do it poorly. Case in point: Bed, Bath & Beyond. In 2023, entering bankruptcy, the ninety-year-old former founders lamented in the *Wall Street Journal,* "If we made an error by not moving fast enough into the internet, it wasn't because we wouldn't spend the money. . . . It was because we goofed."[7] The goof was not recognizing that a Big Bet was needed far earlier, or how to proceed on it. They would have benefited from this book.

The importance of placing Big Bets is empirically backed. McKinsey studied 2,393 of the world's largest corporations to better understand why a select few companies manage to earn more than their cost of capital while most are break-even at best.[8] Central among the findings is that making bold moves is critical to success. Making one or two bold moves more than doubles the odds that a company will move from just covering their cost of capital to becoming a top performer; at three bold moves the odds rise by nearly sixfold. Moreover, "the upside opportunity far outweighs the downside risk," and "making no bold moves is probably the most dangerous strategy of all."[9] A large percentage of Big Bets that are taken fail using typical approaches—but 100 percent of the Big Bet strategies not taken also fail. Look at every company that at one point was healthy, relevant, and had competitive advantages, but is now average. These are companies that failed at Big Bets. These are not counted in the failure percentages reported on Big Bets.

You are holding a book that helps you take more Big Bets because you will be systematically sharper at identifying, shaping, executing, and de-risking the Big Bets before big commitments are made, while creating the most upside potential for the concept.

THE JUNGLE OF AMBIGUITY

The major underlying factor contributing to the high failure rate of transformations is that leaders don't have a clear definition, an actionable goal, a crisp mission creating a defined North Star to galvanize efforts. Once proceeding on the transformation, they fail to isolate this North Star destination and then maintain tight focus on the value creation hypothesis and largest risks, dedicate a team, or create an environment engineered for the needs of the Big Bet. They instead lead with big commitments before the critical risks are tested, adjusted, and validated.

They proceed on Big Bets with a vague, unproven future state definition, adopting a "can't lose" mindset instead of an agile "prove it" style. We want the initiative done, and we want to do it fast, but we don't have a shared, clear, strategic definition of what "it" is or a truly agile risk-forward approach to experiment and prove our bets early. Thus, we work against each other, take long and hard paths, and try to get far too much done, resulting in bloat, conflict, long time frames and a "too big to fail" reality. That is the postmortem summary of most failed transformations and Big Bets.

Big Bets often bog down when the efforts lose momentum or become muddied by other priorities. A critical goal of Big Bet Leadership is to achieve the virtuous balance between maintaining velocity and attacking ambiguity. This requires focusing on the right components of an outcome, and only those components. What routinely pulls organizations out of the virtuous test-and-learn cycle and into the slow, expensive, brittle model is *analysis paralysis*. This is a state of diffused decision making and letting everything be a priority, resulting in complexity, dependencies, and an exponential growth in points of failure. This is the vicious cycle leading to failure in Big Bets.

The Big Bet is bogged down in a jungle morass of ambiguity in which one can hardly move, likely doomed, requiring incredible effort and coordination to make marginal progress. Morale and accountability quickly vanish as everyone senses that the journey to nowhere is under way. Yet, the major system integrators and management consulting firms are more than willing to lead you down this very path. These are the plum engagements that send the armies of young consulting ants marching around your organization, racking up the billable hours.

THE SHORTEST DISTANCE BETWEEN TWO POINTS

To put your Big Bet on the right track, or to turn around an existing strategy, establish a *Big Bet Vector*.

A vector has both a magnitude and a specific direction between two coordinates or points. It is different from just having speed or force in that vectors are directed at specific coordinates. The coordinates here are between the current wicked problem and the exact future state. The magnitude is the speed and constraints applied to prove the feasibility and business value of the coordinates.

Most Big Bets start with a range of definitions and understanding regarding what the real problem, situation, or customer pain is.

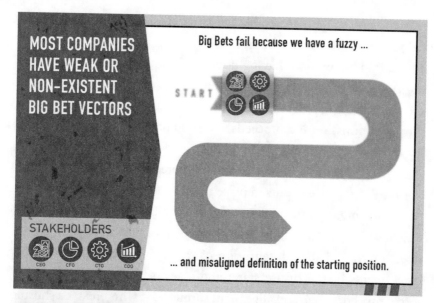

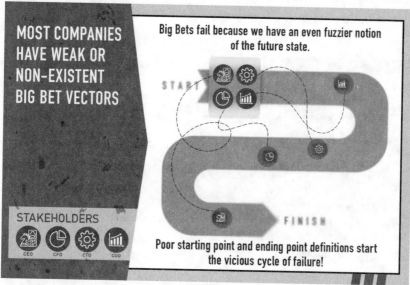

No wonder most Big Bets fail. We don't agree on the precise nature of the wicked problem or existing situation. We don't agree on the future state capability, which is the destination we are targeting. Our team believes they are working together, but they cannot be because of this lack of clarity. Scope expands, validation slows down, the journey to testing gets long and expensive. By the time the value or feasibility is validated, the investment and commitments are often past the point of a comfortable off-ramp. To manage the risk of not delivering, we downsize the ambition of the transformation. We have committed but without having done effective diligence.

A vector is not just speed. Speed can be undirected activity and motion. In Big Bet Leadership, there is a vector that has a defined purpose or mission and proceeds at a rapid pace. This results in velocity and leads the organization to a validated future-state understanding with speed and with alignment to strategy, plans, and priorities.

Big Bet Leadership puts in place the sharp thinking, the nurturing environment, and the low-friction management techniques to clearly define, value, and validate the real problem or customer pain; a precise, smart, and shared definition of the hypotheses for the critical components of the future state; and a set of leadership techniques forcing speed, focus, and alignment throughout. This creates a shorter gap to validating and aligns resources for optimal magnitude of the Big Bet Vector.

With the starting point, which is the wicked problem, firmly defined, the coordinates of the future state are explicitly defined as a hypothesis. Resources are aligned and efficiently deployed. Furthermore, if one tests just the critical valuable and high-risk aspects of the coordinates of the future state, then adjustments can be made deliberately, intentionally, and effectively. This is value-added agility.

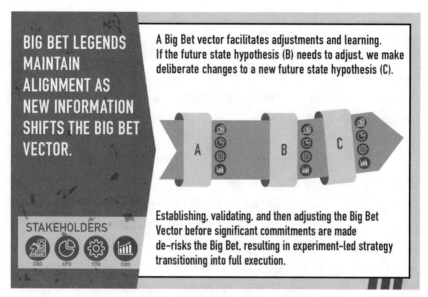

BIG BET LEGENDS MAINTAIN ALIGNMENT AS NEW INFORMATION SHIFTS THE BIG BET VECTOR.

A Big Bet vector facilitates adjustments and learning. If the future state hypothesis (B) needs to adjust, we make deliberate changes to a new future state hypothesis (C).

STAKEHOLDERS

CEO   CFO   CTO   COO

Establishing, validating, and then adjusting the Big Bet Vector before significant commitments are made de-risks the Big Bet, resulting in experiment-led strategy transitioning into full execution.

The *Big Bet Leadership* playbook contains three sections that will help you establish and lead using a Big Bet Vector.

Big Bet Thinking: Change the technique and approach for rapidly understanding the wicked problem and defining your critical hypothesis for the future state. In other words, create crystal clarity around the starting and end points of your Big Bet Vector. You won't think about strategy, envisioning, and problem-solving the same way you used to.

Big Bet Environment: Create optimal conditions with the essential checklist for the journey, giving your Big Bet the best chances to succeed. Doing this addresses some of the major failure points of transformations, which result from unwillingness to change the resources, policies, or constraints for the purpose of the Big Bet Vector. Create a clean-slate environment without the bureaucracy and entanglements of the existing organization.

Big Bet Management: Senior executives need to lead to impactful upside outcomes while guarding against the natural enemies of change. In this section we navigate the high-stakes decisions and failure points of the journey. Protect against the forces pulling against progress by maintaining the velocity of the Big Bet Vector.

THE CRITICAL HABITS OF BIG BET LEGENDS

What is it that Big Bet legends like Jeff Bezos, Elon Musk, Satya Nadella, and John Legere do differently? How do they tilt the odds in their favor to consistently deliver trajectory-changing results while others so regularly fail? Getting one Big Bet right might be chalked up to luck. Getting a series of them right is something different. These Big Bet legends act in ways that Big Bet losers do not. Big Bet legends have three consistent, critical leadership techniques:

Create clarity. Guided by a deep curiosity about the customer, a clear vision of critical use cases and features, and a strong grasp of the underlying first principles, the masters of Big Bets consistently reject vague notions of future-state transformations. Failing to escape the fog of war can spell disaster. Successful leaders continuously identify the most significant sources of ambiguity and risk, pinpointing precise use cases, operational requirements, and the core of customer needs. By doing so, they unite their teams in the pursuit of systematic elimination and circumvention of uncertainty.

Maintain velocity. Big Bet legends have a keen sense of what should move fast and what takes time to design, engineer, and build. They know that material risk is added to the concept through analysis paralysis, which is the comfortable pace that successful and large companies operate in. Big Bet leaders create machinery and cultures that value speed and early rapid learning. Velocity decreases the risk of status quo approaches, bloated initiatives, and major failure from infiltrating the Big Bet.

Prioritize risk and value. Big Bet legends accelerate fast and efficient testing and validation on the high-risk, high-value points. They conversely defer and delay any scope that is not high-risk and high-value.

They exhibit an unwavering commitment to preventing themselves and their teams from being sidetracked or overwhelmed by noncritical tasks or factors. Big Bet legends possess a keen understanding of what is genuinely challenging, as opposed to issues that unnecessarily complicate matters. They attack large and valuable markets and customer needs. They combat bureaucracy, ensuring that only Big Bet priorities take precedence. As Bezos once advised John Rossman, "Don't let simple things become the hard things. Only let hard things be the hard things." This is setting priorities.

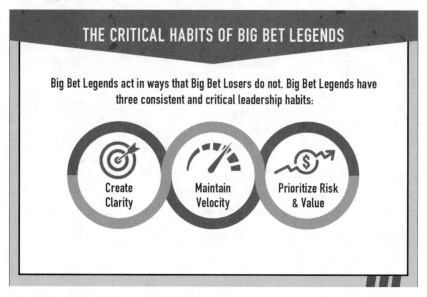

THE CRITICAL HABITS OF BIG BET LEGENDS

Big Bet Legends act in ways that Big Bet Losers do not. Big Bet Legends have three consistent and critical leadership habits:

Create Clarity

Maintain Velocity

Prioritize Risk & Value

Throughout our exploration of tackling wicked problems with Big Bet Leadership, those three critical habits consistently emerge as vital. These foundational principles of Big Bet Leadership form the cornerstone of a genuine Big Bet Vector by articulating a crystal-clear vision of future capabilities, rigorously testing, validating with speed and discipline, and safeguarding the mission from forces that threaten to muddle objectives, decelerate progress, or minimize the ambition.

YOUR BIG BET

Pause for a moment and consider the following questions. Perhaps do this as a leadership team:

As a company, how successful is your digital transformation journey? Has your organization emerged as a systematic innovator cranking out innovative products leading to a great financial return? Have you secured a sustainable competitive edge? Do you excel in unlocking value and efficiency through the intelligent application of disruptive technologies and AI? Is your cost and operating structure an advantage for your business? Are you prepared to achieve the business growth and financial targets set forth? Is the company playing it too safe?

As a professional, does your career revolve around a Big Bet? Is your career trajectory tied to a Big Bet? Would you like to be the visionary who tackles wicked problems, forges a competitive advantage, and cultivates a culture of value-based innovation?

If your organization and team are like the vast majority, you are probably contending with these challenges and their related strategies and transformations. At best, you might be making progress but realize there is still considerable opportunity to be created. Acquiring the ability to succeed at Big Bets is a practice that can be honed by leaders and organizations.

Creating a Big Bet Vector by creating clarity, maintaining velocity, and prioritizing risk and value will be your fundamental habits. Let's discuss how to establish the Big Bet Vector and show these habits of Big Bet legends at work by creating memo experiments.

PART I

BIG BET THINKING

"Never be limited by other people's limited imaginations."

—MAE C. JEMISON

As the Chinese proverb wisely suggests, "the journey of a thousand miles begins with a single step." It's precisely at these initial steps, the onset of a Big Bet, where we start to address and rectify the high failure rates. Often, the expert analyses excel in highlighting the numerous inefficiencies of the present state. A wealth of literature supports the need to embrace digital transformation and foster an innovative culture. These works reveal a deep comprehension of our current business and provide compelling examples of where we want to go.

Nevertheless, these opening steps struggle to succinctly and clearly express the user problem, imagine the optimal future state and capability, and rationalize its pursuit. When asked the most important question—"What is the critical problem to solve, and what is the crucial capability that solves this problem?"—diverse answers emerge from the same team, even though they have been collaborating closely. This situation prevails even after months of design efforts and, most critically, even after hefty commitments have been rendered. They don't have a vector. Instead, they have a vague and voluminous set of requirements.

In the Big Bet Thinking chapters, we present a novel approach for defining the fundamental problem and customer pain to be tackled, outlining a crystallized definition of the future capability or use case, explaining its attractiveness, deriving insights from others' experiences, and identifying the critical aspects and risks tied to this future state. Big Bet Thinking lays the groundwork for your Big Bet Vector and begins testing the foundational and highest-risk aspects from the start.

These two chapters outline a set of coordinated techniques, methods, constraints, and objectives to develop the Big Bet Vector. Chapter 1, "Thinking in Outcomes," may seem like it requires a lot of writing, but the underlying principles are to gain a deep understanding of the wicked problem and to find the critical unlock, the essence of a solution, at pace. Chapter 2, "Play Chess, Not Checkers," begins the experimentation and enrichment of this thinking by drawing from other, comparable competitors to improve the understanding of both the wicked problem and the hypothesis of the future state.

In Chapters 1 and 2, we outline a set of memos to write and debate. We believe—and Big Bet legends and research have proven—that for most Big Bet scenarios, writing narratives is the best way to capture and summarize complex business situations, analysis, options, and recommendations and to create the memorable Big Bet Vector. Memos allow for a compelling story to be featured and for subtle but essential characteristics, priorities, and risks to be outlined and communicated. For innovative and complex scenarios, storytelling improves comprehension and recall of the details.

The techniques and results of writing memos can be accomplished with other techniques. We are interested in the clarity of thinking and ability to communicate that to others regardless of how it is achieved. While we outline and articulate this as a set of memos, approaching it by "thinking in pictures" and slides can work.

These are *Big Bet Memo Experiments*. All of these discussed approaches have templates, examples, and tools at https://www. BigBetLeadership.com.

In the Appendix, we give a summary of the research behind our belief that writing memos for complex situations is superior to using slideware and why storytelling is key for novel and memorable ideas.

CHAPTER 1
THINKING IN OUTCOMES

"It is better to be approximately right than precisely wrong."

—WARREN BUFFETT

The most understated and valuable word in business is "done."

Implying a commitment of quality, this word embodies a promise while simultaneously being open to misinterpretation among different parties. It encapsulates numerous meanings, including completed, shipped, adopted, realized, finalized, accepted, approved, goal attained, verified, implemented, signed, committed, and decided. Delivering a completed product satisfying all parties remains a daunting challenge.

All versions of "done" represent an important result—a clear and unarguable resolution. "Done" must be unambiguous, implying that the work undertaken has been successfully accomplished and can now facilitate the pursuit of the next goal on the to-do list. The concept of "done" is not a terminus or a final word, but an enabler for transitioning to the next step. Onward!

What are the business challenges, transformations, innovations, technology initiatives, and difficult problems we would like to call "done"? The business needs to deliver innovative products, services, and business models to differentiate from their competition and grow margins. Our customers need to be successful with our products and services if we hope to retain their trust and business. We need to finish the elusive mission of digital transformation. We need our Big Bet strategies to deliver results matching the business case justifying them—or better.

Getting to "done" on our Big Bet strategies has proven to be almost impossible for most Big Bets.

What's more, even "done" is not the optimal outcome. Ideally, we want to pair "done" with another attribute—"fast."

No executive has ever said, "I wish I needed to hire more management consultants" or "I wish this digital transformation took longer." Leaders always want to get the right results—*faster*. We seek success in our Big Bet initiatives as quickly and efficiently as possible. We want to get to done, fast.

But the seemingly impossible challenge is how? Are we going to continue to plan, budget, approve, manage, and struggle with these business imperatives with all the many proven leadership, strategy, and program methods of the past? Are we going to use the same tools we've always used and cross our fingers and hope for different results this time?

Peter Drucker said, "If you want something new, you have to stop doing something old."[1]

Get to done, fast with a robust leadership philosophy, techniques, and mindset. This playbook opens with *Thinking in Outcomes*. Successful Big Bets use a systematic leadership approach of working future-back, risk-forward. By Thinking in Outcomes from the very beginning, a clear Big Bet Vector is established. You will get to done, fast.

A MASTER CLASS IN OUTCOME DEFINITIONS

The nuances of Thinking in Outcomes become embedded into your leadership style. Thinking in Outcomes is complemented with a set of approaches but is much more an attitude and logical questioning technique than a methodology. Here's where our story starts—in attitude.

John tells this story:

> In 2002, I joined Amazon as the Director of Merchant Integration. Our mission was to add millions of items (SKUs), and thousands of sellers (aka merchants) in retail categories beyond books, music, and video. But it started out slowly.
>
> In early 2003, with less than a year under my belt, I was still considered the new guy on the block. I was sitting in a conference room in the company's Seattle headquarters, surrounded by what's called the S-Team, a group that includes Amazon's twenty most senior executives, and I happened to be the center of attention. Unfortunately, this was because the founder and CEO, Jeff Bezos, was frustrated. All eyes turned in my direction when Jeff asked me a deceptively simple question: "How many merchants have launched since the first of the year?"
>
> The question puzzled me since, at that moment, there simply weren't any third-party merchants to launch. The number was outside my direct control. A bit apologetically, I responded, "Well, you see, as of right now—" Before I could finish, Jeff erupted, "The answer to that question begins with a number!"
>
> I hesitated, frantically juggling possible responses in my head. Finally, taking a big gulp, I offered the simple answer he was asking for: "Six, but—"
>
> Jeff pounced like a lion tearing into the soft underbelly of its kill. "That is the most pathetic answer I have ever heard!" The ensuing rant was an educational exercise, using this situation as an opportunity

to set an example and to transmit a series of cultural, strategic, and operational messages to the leaders of the company. The lecture was classic Jeff because it contained valuable lessons about expectations and how we got things done at Amazon.

Jeff didn't want an explanation; he wanted to start with a clear answer, and then he would decide where to take the conversation. He wanted to start with the outcome. In this particular case, Jeff wanted to tell me, to tell everyone, to "Act Like an Owner," which is the second of Amazon's leadership principles.

Bezos wanted a particular outcome in his leaders. He wanted them to act like owners. In that moment, he was thinking in outcomes. Even though John's title was Director of Merchant Integration and many dependent functions for the Marketplace business did not report to him, Bezos expected John to ignore commonly respected conventions like job titles and formal organizational charts and run the Marketplace business. He didn't care about the organization structure; he cared about outcomes.

John didn't need to be told twice—lesson learned. From that day forward, he acted like an owner and focused on driving to the best possible outcome, not just the scope of his direct organization.

One way we can see this process at work is to look at the way John approached the creation of the Amazon Marketplace business. At the start, John made a specific, concrete move that demonstrated the act of Thinking in Outcomes: he helped write a memo for Amazon Marketplace. Amazon referred to this type of memo as a future press release.

"A seller, in the middle of the night, can register, list an item, receive an order, and delight a customer as though Amazon the retailer had done it."

It was a simple sentence, but it set the bar high for a seller and customer experience in vivid and minimalist terms. It articulated both the superior customer experience, the self-service seller experience, and the combined Amazon and merchant accountabilities to deliver a differentiated and trusted customer experience. As the project's outcome vision, it imposed specific requirements on both Amazon and their sellers. The project would be complex. Just to deliver self-service registration, several different systems had to be integrated.

To guard against losing velocity and clarity, John used the press release as a forcing function to compel all these teams, none of which reported directly to him, to get this hard work done. He used this to develop the merchant integration guide and explicit operating mandates and obligations for sellers. This large project consisted of Amazon engineering, customer service, product management, and business development plus about forty large apparel brands for the initial November 2002 launch of the apparel category. He avoided misalignment and scope creep and launched quickly, in about six months, because the teams were able to act nimbly and focus on an outcome. The outcome statement acted as the North Star, the killer feature, galvanizing focus and clarity across a large stakeholder group by using influence and not control.

DESIGNING YOUR BIG BET WITH OUTCOMES

You're in! You're ready to have the outcome superpower added to your toolkit. How do you lead and structure to Think in Outcomes?

To create or formulate the Big Bet scenario, there are three core activities:

- First, the customer, problem, and market exploration analysis.

- Second, the outcome definition design.

- Third, the outcome financial analysis.

Although each of these activities, analyses, and corresponding memos might appear as sequential, they are highly iterative and typically simultaneous. The work is best done with one small team simultaneously doing all three of these. This is where the magic happens—the insight, the idea, or as we will talk about, the killer feature, and the privileged cost structure are revealed.

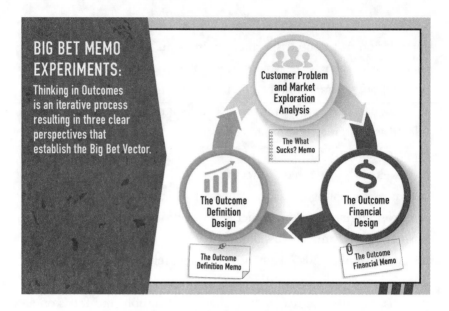

BIG BET MEMO EXPERIMENTS: Thinking in Outcomes is an iterative process resulting in three clear perspectives that establish the Big Bet Vector.

Throughout *Big Bet Leadership*, we reference several well-understood approaches or methodologies, such as "the jobs to be done" methodology or Objectives and Key Results (OKRs). We often either introduce a new approach or concept specifically to assist in Big Bets, or as a point of emphasis and constraint on an existing approach.

The importance is the philosophy and insight, the desired impact described, not the specific analysis approach or technique. As the saying goes, you must run the right horse for the right course. In the case of Big Bets, the circumstances of the situation dictate the specific tools to be used.

THE CUSTOMER, WICKED PROBLEM, AND MARKET EXPLORATION ANALYSIS

Problems, challenges, and opportunities come in all shapes, sizes, and orientations. Our customers have a problem. Our cost structure has a problem. Our technology platform has a problem. We develop a strategy and plan to solve a problem. Deeply understanding the problem and the key stakeholders involved with the problem is key to crafting the right strategy—a plan or policy designed to achieve a major or overall aim. Big Bets start with deeply understanding and deriving the valuable customer pain, the market, or the problem.

One might expect accomplished and high-level business leaders to be outstanding problem-solvers, and thus adept strategists. This assumption proves valid for conventional or easily grasped issues. Nevertheless, when problems become intricate, wicked, concealed, and multi-layered, compounded by constraints curbing our available options and the unavoidable challenge that the leaders themselves are part of the situation, numerous business leaders falter in wicked problem-solving and, subsequently, strategic formulation. Big Bets, which arise at all tiers of an organization, involve tackling significant, complex, valuable, and high-risk problems that call for creative, world-class problem-solving expertise and strategy formulation.

The difficulty is not rooted in an absence of expertise; the true obstacle is that expertise frequently carries with it filters and biases limiting the capacity to view problems or solutions from diverse standpoints, thereby hindering the formation of resourceful and all-encompassing strategies. Pinpointing the crux of the issue—the singular point of leverage that reveals value, exposes a new market, or uncovers a novel competitive edge—defines strategy. In essence, strategy and problem-solving are one and the same.

There are several helpful methodologies and frameworks. If the situation is "I need to develop a better solution for my end business user," then the "jobs to be done" methodology might be the right methodology. If the problem is a response to a competitive threat posed by a new market entrant, then a strengths, weaknesses, opportunities, and threats (SWOT) analysis might be helpful.

Independent of the technique or methodology utilized, our quest revolves around a few essential discoveries. We need to pinpoint the customer and comprehend their specific pain point, challenge, or unaddressed requirement. What is a clever approach, a hypothesis for the exceptional feature that resolves this issue? This is a distinguishing aspect of Thinking in Outcomes. Instead of enumerating and attempting to prioritize every need or requirement, we concentrate on a clear, unique capability that our analysis, customer curiosity, and business intuition indicate will lead to a decisive advantage and financial return. What do they, or their boss, really want done?

We term this the killer feature.[2] Although expressed as a lone characteristic, the killer feature may manifest as a killer use case, killer value proposition, or a killer application supported by a collection of capabilities enabling it.

THE CUSTOMER PAIN POINT: WHAT SUCKS?

We have developed a unique framework to address these questions to circumvent expertise bias and expedite the process of pinpointing a hypothesis addressing the core issue. This is sparked by posing a provocative and candid question: What sucks? The question "What sucks?" encourages critical analysis and aids in uncovering valuable customer needs or challenges that may have previously gone unnoticed.

Tackling a minor inconvenience to a customer or an operational irritation is not expected to produce noteworthy outcomes. In contrast, rectifying a truly problematic and vexing concern—one that customers are inclined to change providers for and invest in—holds the key to establishing a unique selling point and fostering value creation.

The customer, wicked problem, and market exploration analysis has two clear goals: identify a key unmet customer need or pain point and create a killer feature to address it. That's it. If you can walk in and on day one nail this, proceed! We are always looking to accelerate. But in most cases you can't, or there are multiple perspectives on the answer. It takes work, curiosity, expertise, diversity, and likely many iterations to come to one best perspective.

The notion of a killer feature is key. A killer feature is a term used to describe an extraordinary or unique feature in a product, service, or technology, allowing it to stand out from its competitors and giving a significant competitive advantage. This feature is often considered the primary reason and rationale for customers to choose and pay for that product or service over others in the market. Subtle feature differentiations, small cost differences, or slightly different value propositions will not entice target customers to switch to a product or service, create a new product category, or create the organizational momentum to transform. Minor improvements do not result in differentiated businesses. The killer feature is why customers will love the solution, and why the organization will change—stated as a hypothesis.

The *Big Bet What Sucks Memo*[3] accelerates a structured manner of exploring the problem space, getting us to deeper insights on customers and the experiences they deserve, perhaps even when they aren't aware of the pain. We do this in a faster, repeatable manner, assisting in better thinking and a deeper understanding of our customers.

Let's look at the memo in an abbreviated and fictitious example representing an authentically painful and limiting business challenge.

"It sucks when . . . a company is locked in with a single cloud provider for its technology platform."

A high percentage of enterprises will likely identify with this predicament, restriction, and pain point.

Your company depends on a cloud provider for technology operations and services. While the cloud platform has been advantageous, your contract with your cloud vendor is beginning to show signs of wear, and expenses are rapidly piling up. It might not deliver the specific capabilities, such as a unique security feature or access to a pioneering AI model. Enterprising, affordable, and aggressive suppliers have surfaced and are vying for your business, offering an opportunity for reducing cloud expense. But . . . retrofitting your current technology would require a massive platform undertaking. Your negotiating power with your existing provider is minimal, as they understand the complexities of transitioning. You are locked in, and being locked in is a truly wicked problem and valuable customer pain point!

When we have identified the heart of the problem, the next step is to identify for whom it sucks the most within the organization.

These are the actors, and understanding the issue through real people and roles is key to our analysis and storytelling. In this case, let's focus on two actors.

The chief information officer (CIO) holds a crucial position in any organization, bearing the responsibility of delivering a return from technology investments and ensuring seamless business operations. This top-tier executive aims to accelerate the deployment of new capabilities while simultaneously maintaining a forward-looking approach, creating flexibility and agility for the future.

The second actor is the cloud architect or software engineer. This individual uses the cloud infrastructure to operate customer and business solutions. It is great when one primary vendor offers all the services. But the job becomes a nightmare when the vendor cannot offer a needed capability—or if they can, their prices are higher than a different provider in the space.

How often does vendor lock-in make trouble for the enterprise? Annually, the CIO must answer for the high-priced vendor or create budget flexibility. It is a problem measured in dollars. The issue also surfaces over years when rival cloud providers offer better pricing or service levels. You cannot take advantage of that because you are locked in.

If this vendor lock-in did not exist, the company could reap substantial benefits, such as

- Having access to cutting-edge services such as AI models or security services.

- Being able to test different services offered by various cloud providers.

- Realizing lower costs and better terms for the cloud computing.

- Architecting true technology agility, enabling the business to react to the market faster.

Now, frame, reframe, and re-reframe the problem. Reframing the problem three to five times helps us slow down, see the expanse of the problem, and prevent us from rushing forward with the first words that come to mind.

In our example, we asked "What's the real problem?" four times, working to a deeper understanding:

The problem is I have no leverage with my cloud vendors.

Why? Because it is complex and prohibitively expensive and time consuming to switch providers, and they know it.

Why? Because they built the architecture and they know it is custom per provider, and they require that my integrations be custom written to work.

Why? Because technology architectures and mechanisms are tightly coupled to the services and cloud providers.

Why? Because dynamic cloud service switching has not been invented.

The core issue lies not with the cloud providers themselves, but rather with the technology integration methods, standards, and outdated architectures. If a system for dynamic, flexible cloud service usage were created, it could resolve the cloud vendor lock-in dilemma.

Consequently, the hypothesis for a game-changing killer feature would be as follows: a technology platform enabling dynamic, real-time switching between cloud services, allowing for the pricing and utilization of various cloud computing services to be managed instantaneously across multiple computing platforms.

Consider the immense potential of that game-changing feature. Wouldn't you be intrigued by a service enabling real-time dynamic pricing and utilization of cloud computing services? Even more crucially, we have not weighed down the Big Bet with hundreds of supplementary requirements or concepts. This groundbreaking feature is a hypothesis—we believe this is the key future capability that will attract new customers.

With our killer feature, it's time to proceed to the Outcomes Definition Memo.

THE OUTCOME DEFINITION MEMO

Using the killer feature statement as the starting input, the *Big Bet*

Outcome Definition Memo consists of a robust articulation, the full framing, of the critical, limited and often hard-to-achieve aspects and key constraints to deliver this killer feature.

The Big Bet Outcome Definition Memo includes these three key elements:

The killer feature—derived from the customer and problem exploration work from the What Sucks Memo.

The value proposition for this outcome—a short statement communicating why a buyer would purchase your product or service. It is written to the customer, understands the pains and gains the customer experiences, and proposes a solution.

The high-risk operating imperatives—the key and difficult operating objectives required by the customer or the company for which key innovations are needed, or risks exist. These often include cost, quality, features, throughput, or unit cost targets. To enforce prioritization, no more than five operating imperatives are included.

The objective of the Outcome Definition Memo is to focus exclusively on the essential, valuable, and high-risk elements to empower the game-changing feature within a new product, service, or capability.

Here is the fictional Big Bet Outcome Definition Memo, written as a story, for our cloud vendor lock-in scenario.

Ten Billion Dollars Saved for Corporate CIOs with Dynamic Optimized Cloud Load Balancing

CloudPicker Enterprises announced that over the past year they have saved their clients $10 billion USD in verified cloud expenses while actually improving redundancy, security, and performance. Through the patented cloud-step-optimizer-network-agent, dynamic real-time workload allocation is made based on client-specified cost, performance, and business rules optimization.

In legacy gen-1 cloud provider architecture, corporate IT organizations had to pick and architect applications and workloads to the cloud provider that would service them. Although design patterns and tools such as container technology helped make portability feasible, it was still extremely complex and NEVER dynamically done based on spot compute pricing and other business rules to optimize cost and performance. With cloud computing being a $1T annual spend for US corporate technology growing at 20% a year, this lock-in was yet another "vendor wins" situation.

We win when our customers win. And our customers win when there is dynamic competition to serve corporate customers the best. Total customer growth grew 50% YOY, and more importantly, in customers using CloudPicker for more than 18 months, over 90% of their total "share of cloud" is processed through the CloudAuctionOptimizer service. Latency for workloads improves by 10% and saves, on average, 19.5% over current prices.

Clara Von Fokker, founder and CEO of CloudPicker, states "We are thrilled to help free corporate IT from lock-in to the old gen-1 cloud providers. Open competition is critical to fair and open business competition. We've seen five new cloud providers achieve market success because they now can compete.

"We've been able to improve our mission of helping out in disasters because of CloudPicker," states Hal McGregor, CIO of the American Red Cross. "Our technology performance is vital to our mission. Not only did the speed of our technology applications improve, but we were able to shift 20% of our IT budget to actually serving those impacted by disasters."

Key Features:

Set and forget—once workloads are ported and optimization rules are configured, there are no ongoing CloudPicker operations.

Zero dependencies—once workloads are ported and certified, there are zero dependencies on any cloud provider.

Administrators required, not teams of architects and developers—Using CloudPicker does not require programmers, system architects, or system integrators. Your current system administrators can do everything required by CloudPicker.

The CloudPicker Outcome Definition Memo is fiction—but sounds like a great business! This Outcome Definition Memo helps us not only understand the customer and the killer feature, but the story that might be told, making this memorable. It brings to life the way the real solution might appear in the real world, heralded by customers. It's the human factor and emotion that helps everyone see themselves in the story.

So far we have explored the customer and what sucks. We have defined a killer feature, fleshed out the value proposition, and framed the key complementary high-risk requirements of a concept. Do we have our Big Bet Vector with a clear understanding of the problem and a precise definition of the future state? Almost. Let us see if the juice is worth the squeeze.

A BIG BET MUST BE WORTH IT

Done correctly, the Big Bet Outcome Definition Memo features keen insights and definitions—a killer feature delivering a dramatic improvement in the customer value proposition. It identifies step change improvements to key operating imperatives complementing or required to deliver that killer feature. If the customer value propositions, killer feature, and high-risk operational imperatives are achieved, surely the result will be the financial impact expected of a Big Bet, right?

Maybe.

The *Big Bet Outcome Financial Memo* inspires innovation and confidence in our ability to create a thriving business based on this future state capability. Naturally, your organization can only engage in a limited number of Big Bets simultaneously. It's crucial to concentrate organizational efforts and resources on those Big Bets with the potential to deliver transformative financial results in line with the capability impact. Here's how to complement the Outcomes Definition with a corresponding financial innovation and economic advantage.

WRITING YOUR BIG BET OUTCOME FINANCIAL MEMO

While analysis paralysis takes center stage as the foremost nemesis during the outcome definition design process, false precision claims the same title when it comes to conducting outcome financial projections.

The Big Bet Outcome Financial Memo tackles false precision by shifting the focus from the minutiae of a spreadsheet financial model to the narrative that elucidates the financial model. Crafting the memo to highlight the essential elements of the financial model sidesteps the pitfalls associated with conventional business case exercises.

When building a business case or financial model, organizations commonly scrutinize the assumptions feeding into the business case, only to later regard the resulting outputs as established facts. Teams evaluate the examined ROI against other initiatives to prioritize, as though the ROIs being compared are indisputable. They then modify revenue and expenditure forecasts based on these business case outputs. Teams leverage the validation of their exponential growth projections to advocate for substantial, early-stage investments in fundamental capabilities, aiming to seize fleeting opportunities or secure first-mover advantages.

We are playing business-case-forecasting roulette, encouraging wildly inaccurate and optimistic forecasts, while not surfacing and focusing on the critical assumptions or risks.

So, what is the correct response? Should you enlist teams of consultants and financial planning analysts to augment the diligence of the business case until you have banished all vagueness from your Big Bet financial forecast? Not recommended! In doing so, you would only swap false precision for its comrade, analysis paralysis. The priceless insights and revelatory moments dissipate, replaced with additional time and effort when the workload is distributed among various teams. The target is to navigate ambiguity while sustaining pace. The formula for success is a subtle yet impactful reimagining of the intent within the Outcome Financial Design exercise, as compared to traditional business case approaches.

The Big Bet Outcome Financial Design and Memo reorients the approach:

From believing that building a base of expected financial outcomes validating the financial prize is worth the effort, while feeding into vital decisions such as comparing projects, allocating resources, budgeting, and more. This perspective triggers the hazardous journey toward truly "betting big" as overestimation, budgeting, and business case bravado take over.

To identifying the limited and essential factors for the gains to merit the effort by designing an array of financial targets and constraints for verification. Work toward verifying these "what would have to be true" financial assumptions, and then either expand or discontinue the Big Bet proposal. By centering on the premise that foretelling the future is infeasible, but developing proof points is entirely doable, it is possible to circumvent business case bravado and steep growth forecasts.

The approach difference is subtle, and thus easy to adopt, but creates a stark culture contrast. The typical scenario implicitly assumes that ambiguity is eliminated around the financial profile of an early-stage Big Bet idea through an upfront business case exercise—typically true for incremental bets and well understood scenarios, but not true for wicked problems and Big Bets.

The Big Bet Outcome Financial Memo confronts uncertainty, acknowledging the essence of a bet—that there are numerous risks with no instant means to eradicate them. Rather than shy away and hide the risks, we highlight and emphasize the primary sources of ambiguity, tackling them head-on with a mentality rooted in experimentation and innovation. By bringing clarity to the key areas of uncertainty and fostering a leadership style embracing the inherent nature of experimentation, we preserve momentum, challenge ambiguity, and pursue financial ingenuity.

Tactically, we recommend these steps in writing your Big Bet Outcome Financial Memo:

Build a reverse income statement. The reverse income statement methodology—developed as a component of Design Driven Planning—is a great application of Thinking in Outcomes and was a central inspiration behind the techniques championed by Eric Ries in his book *The Lean Startup*.[4] Using reverse income statements, the overall goal is to define a future version of the financial statement behind your Big Bet idea, starting with the compelling financial outcome you seek to achieve. Then work back to define the income statement line items to get there. The reverse income statement should capture the set of high-level financial assumptions for both benefits and costs that, if achieved, would result in the juice being worth the squeeze.

Create a Big Bet Outcome Financial Memo. Include the following elements:

Opportunity sizing—In this section, in narrative form, articulate the top three results that must be true for the "juice to be worth the squeeze." Keep it to three to avoid analysis paralysis and confusion. For market-oriented Big Bets—for example, a new business unit—this section outlines why the market size is big enough to support Big Bet impact. This is usually a combination of large and/or fast-growing markets. For new markets, the emphasis is on identifying significant pain points for large customer bases.

For internal initiatives—perhaps a digital transformation or a large technology program—identify the top three sources of value creation with a tangible degree of clarity. For example, drive revenue through reduced churn by improving three specific customer experiences, or reduce customer acquisition costs by a targeted amount through a list of enumerated capabilities.

Key cost structure innovation—Big Bets eventually consume significant resources. Additionally, market-oriented Big Bets attract the attention of competitors looking to replicate the customer value proposition. While it's not 100 percent required, Big Bets featuring an innovation delivering a step-change improvement to the cost structure of the bet are more likely to avoid debilitating slowdowns during the critically important scaling phase as they wait for resources to become available. They are more likely to be able to invest to maintain their competitiveness in the market once launched, and they have a positive cash flow much earlier in scaling, allowing for more options to either measure or accelerate expansion.

From the very beginning, we recommend a section in your Big Bet Outcome Financial Memo articulating the cost structure innovation to fuel the financial success of your Big Bet. This isn't something that naturally pops out of the opportunity sizing exercise, and yet it's great to capture early.

Elon Musk and his related companies often use a dramatic reduction in cost as the killer feature. SpaceX reduced the variable cost of rocket launches to roughly $1,200 per pound of payload to reach low-Earth orbit. NASA's now retired Space Shuttle program had a cost of $30,000 per pound.[5] The Boring Company, which creates tunnels to alleviate traffic, reduced the cost per mile of tunneling from $1 billion–$2 billion per mile to $10 million per mile.[6] Tesla has a best-in-industry profit advantage, estimated at $9,574 per vehicle compared to GM, in second place, at $2,150.[7] Musk continues to apply cost pressure on the established auto industry. "There is a clear path to making a . . . smaller vehicle that is roughly half the production cost and difficulty of our Model 3."[8]

Top costs to control—While sections one and two of your Big Bet Outcome Financial Memo articulate the exciting features of your reverse income statement, such as sources of trajectory-changing growth and an innovative cost structure, section three is about the mundane. There are times when mundane elements of a cost structure sneak up on a Big Bet idea and kill it. These mundane elements can include overhead costs, input or raw material prices, customer care, or marketing efficiency. You may not need industry-beating performance in any of those areas to succeed—but you also cannot afford to allow elements of your cost structure to balloon in the background.

In this part of the narrative, simply identify the top five elements of the cost structure to monitor in order to ensure they are what we like to call "beautifully average." Again, the point isn't to deliver "great" but simply to make sure the organization isn't so focused on growth and cost structure innovation that these otherwise seemingly unimportant line items team up to sink the idea.

Articulate up to five cost drivers and what it will take to ensure they stay within reasonable limits. The result is a readable memo explaining in simple sentences the key sources of financial ambiguity of your Big Bet, balancing the value-added analysis with velocity. You are in an advantageous position to move forward.

An example of innovating a killer customer feature and business model with a cost advantaged innovation is the Amazon Delivery Service Partner program. The "last mile of delivery" has been the financial choke point on many businesses. Labor, capital costs, operating complexity, and legal risks would all feed into the financial analysis and solution design. Amazon executives likely started with a set of financial "cost per order" metric objectives to complement the killer feature of same-day delivery for millions of different items and asked, "How do we innovate a model and solve for this?" Their answer—develop an on-demand independent, yet branded operator-owned model.[9]

A financial edge is as crucial to the success of an innovative idea as its game-changing features and use case are, if not more so. Southwest

Airlines is an example of a company that has differentiated itself through an innovative cost model. Operating a single type of aircraft, having a point-to-point flight model, using secondary and lower-cost airports, employing a direct sales model, and providing a no-frills customer experience are five of the innovations behind their cost model. How big of an advantage do they have? Southwest Airlines has an approximate 25% cost structure advantage, as measured by cost per available mile (CASM), compared to its primary competition.

Warren Buffett, the Oracle of Omaha, recognizes the importance of cost structure innovation. "The most important thing [is] trying to find a business with a wide and long-lasting moat around it . . . protecting a terrific economic castle with an honest lord in charge of the castle."[10] Build a formidable economic castle with your Big Bet by applying sufficient focus on this often-underdeveloped aspect of innovation.

BACK TO DONE, FAST

In leading the efforts of your Thinking in Outcomes activities and the development of a Big Bet Memo Experiments, what are the key risks to be aware of? The dangers are setting a slow pace, falling into the trap of false precision, and not developing viable options or variations, creating bias for the one version of the future outcome. The consistent challenge is in preventing all the reasons why big organizations are slow and typically incremental in their innovations—drag, bureaucracy, excuses, complexity, misguided traditions, and organization structure. This is analysis paralysis and bureaucracy.

Constraints on both the depth and duration of development avoid these risks.

To guard against these potholes, give any one set of Big Bet Memo Experiments no more than three weeks for development—hopefully much less than that, like a day or two. We are optimizing for a killer feature with rough sketches beyond it without trying to figure out the details of scope, delivery, or financial estimates. The best scenarios are done by developing several concept memos concurrently in a rapid, focused, multi-day workshop.

The spirit and tone applied in both the development and review of this work, how a team works together to do this, and how these memos are debated and used is key. When you're dealing in Big Bets, Thinking in Outcomes is critical, but it is not the only underpinning of a successful Big Bet. Thinking in Outcomes provides focus, clarity, and choice. Thinking in Outcomes is best done at the beginning of a Big Bet, but can be done at a midpoint to create simplification and focus for an existing situation.

What can we learn from others to improve our thinking? How do we start iterating and actually testing our concepts? Let's play a game.

CHAPTER 2
PLAY CHESS, NOT CHECKERS

"When you see a good move, look for a better one."

—EMANUEL LASKER

To hear some tell it, Bill Gates "stole" the graphical user interface operating system from Steve Jobs and Apple.

Or did Steve Jobs steal it first from Xerox PARC?

In another story, Bill Gates stole the operating system contract with IBM from his partner Gary Kildall. Kildall was founder at Digital Research, Inc. (DRI) makers of CP/M—Control Program for Microcomputers, an early PC operating system. Did that happen? Did Kildall miss his chance at the contract by opting to take his personal airplane out for a spin rather than meeting with IBM officials? Or was Gates just opportunistic in snagging the IBM deal and crafting the phrase "Gary went flying"[1] to stand evermore as the industry's metaphor for a missed opportunity?

All these statements are simplistic and miss the mark. We all build on the work of others.

Bill Gates knew that Apple was working on an operating system based on a graphical user interface, as Microsoft was supplying Apple with early version of MS Word and MS Excel and the Apple team showed it to them. Gates and Jobs both drew inspiration from the early demos of the Xerox graphical user interface. And Gates saw an opportunity for Microsoft to expand into operating systems with the IBM opportunity in 1988.

But nobody stole anything.

In each case, Gates and Jobs took the core of a concept, and innovated—not just creating an innovative technology, but a new business model and new ecosystem. They did not steal. They observed, intuited the future market, devised a powerful business model, and built the combination of products, partners, and distribution to shape an industry.

While the industry was playing checkers—thinking in the moment—Gates and Jobs were playing chess.

A successful Big Bet, like the ones made by Bill Gates and Steve Jobs, is the result of a particular aspect of high-level chess play: the ability to imagine multiple moves ahead. When you can see the whole board of your marketplace and envision how each of your moves might create a new ecosystem of play in your industry, you can make the Big Bets that your competitors may not even be able to imagine until it is too late.

This type of innovation is not a matter of genius; it is a process that can be learned and followed.

Let us begin by looking at the master's work.

In the case of Microsoft's work with DOS and then the Windows operating system, there were at least four important moves executed by the company's leadership:

- Seized the opportunity to build the operating system for IBM in 1980. The first choice for the job was Bill Gates's close business partner, Gary Kildall at DRI—who, as legend has it, went flying on the wrong day and is now a footnote in PC history.[2]

- Licensed an early version of DOS to deliver this operating system, from a then-little-known and now forgotten company named Seattle Computer Products.[3] This allowed Microsoft to deliver the IBM operating system at a time when Microsoft did not have their own operating systems. The contract with Seattle Computer Products allowed Microsoft to both improve upon and resell the application named DOS without further royalties to Seattle Computer Products.

- Negotiated a clause to the contract with IBM that gave Microsoft the rights to sell DOS to other original equipment manufacturers (OEMs) in the computer industry.

- Understood that the primary value for a future industry was not the physical PC, but the cross-platform combination of a standard chip-based architecture and the operating system that could operate across the standard chip-based architecture. This was Bill Gates's vision. He imagined the eventual outcome of "a PC on every desk and in every home"[4] and the business applications for PCs. Trusting that, he put together the moves to seize the control and value that were to come. He saw the future vision of an Intel-based CPU PC world and the portable opportunity to be the platform for that entire ecosystem, which became known as Wintel.[5] Meanwhile, the rest of the computer industry was busy playing checkers, thinking one product, one feature at a time.

How did he get so lucky?

The saying goes that "luck is the intersection of preparation and opportunity." So, if you want to get lucky, you need to prepare and create opportunities. You need to de-risk and accelerate your Big Bet.

We have learned this is possible by employing a combination of reverse engineering and systems thinking.

Let's look more closely at that duo.

OTHER PEOPLE'S OUTCOMES

First moves are often guided by the experience and trajectories of others. They may be pillars of eras past. Or they may be your own current competition. Their stories and data will form the foundations of decision-making and the keys to de-risking efforts.

In his book *Decoding Greatness: How the Best in the World Reverse Engineer Success,*[6] Ron Friedman outlines how greatness is always built on the shoulders of other giants, usually by studying, imitating, benchmarking, breaking down, or in other ways learning in a very directed manner from others. From pharmaceuticals to recipes to sports, imitation is the highest form of compliment, and greatness can be built from it.

The foundation of most exceptional strategies lies in a key component: competitive intelligence, which involves uncovering and learning from the plans and motivations of your rivals and ecosystem. However, competitive intelligence is frequently not implemented at the required pace to directly enhance and refine the crucial insights and outcomes associated with solving vital business issues or formulating high-stakes strategies. As a result, many competitive intelligence efforts guide companies toward incremental improvements rather than facilitating the transformative breakthroughs they seek.

To execute a Big Bet, competitive intelligence with targeted intent and a rapid pace is needed. The intent should make it clear that transformative, not incremental, progress is expected.

When seeking transformative progress, starting from scratch is a losing approach. As Steven Johnson spells out in *Where Good Ideas Come From,*[7] even history's greatest "lightbulb" innovation stories are far more myth than reality. Indeed, the reality is that nearly all breakthrough innovations that succeed at scale are built on a massive foundation of other people's work (OPW). The odds of your Big Bet succeeding are dramatically improved—and the development timeline shortened—when leaders recognize the importance of leveraging OPW and make doing so an explicit step in the process of managing Big Bets.

Indeed, chess masters spend hours studying games already played. They are not stealing or copying—it would be impossible to do so since every live game is a new battlefield of play. Instead, they're internalizing past games to use that learning in new matches. Wins are crafted on the backs of other players' moves.

Leveraging other people's work offers advantages that go beyond expediting your Big Bet by capitalizing on the insights others have already gained. OPW also serves as a potent instrument for shielding your Big Bet from cognitive biases that can give rise to blind spots and flawed assumptions.

Friedman points out that psychologists have long studied the negative effects of staring at a problem for too long, in isolation. The Einstellung effect, mental set, and functional fixedness are all phrases for the same cognitive trap. This is why copying is a good thing, not a bad thing, he notes. It brings other people's thinking into our process and helps us avoid recycling the same old ideas in our heads, over and over. "Far from making us unoriginal, copying breaks the spell. It challenges our assumptions, relaxes our cognitive constraints, and opens us up to new perspectives," he says.[8]

BENCHMARKING OUTCOMES

All ideas and approaches can benefit from studying history and competitors. For Big Bets, a focused approach balancing speed with valuable insights is needed. For that, we have developed a framework to systematize the approach. We call it *Other People's Outcomes*. This technique allows teams to de-risk, accelerate the initial concept, and actually test the ideas in their Big Bet Memo Experiments by leveraging what we can quickly learn from others.

Here is how the *Big Bet Other People's Outcome Memo"* is developed:

Begin with the Big Bet Memo Experiments. Then, identify three competitor or analogous commercial offerings for the capability that you might be able to learn from.

Use the same approaches from the prior analysis, but put the competitor offering instead of your own idea through the framework. These reverse engineered and benchmarked strategies are captured in the Big Bet Other People's Outcome Memo.

It might look like this: Perhaps as a major grocery chain, your Outcome Definition Memo is focused on radically improving the "buy online and pick up in store" (BOPIS) use case. In this scenario, your killer feature envisions the store associate bringing customer-recommended and "goes-with" items in the delivery cart that is wheeled to the customer car, along with the items ordered by the customer. You envision an up-sale conversion rate justifying the logistical efforts to enable. The average order size increases 20%, boosting order profitability by 40%, as many of the "goes-with" items are high-margin items such as prepared foods, gourmet items, and beverages.

That's your killer feature. Now, from whom can we learn more about this?

In this scenario, a sensible approach is doing benchmark analysis on the best grocery sector competitor offering a leading buy online, pick up in store capability. But do not stop at just a great direct competitor. Study the best non-grocery retailer who does BOPIS, and the best restaurant BOPIS operator. Complete the first iteration of these quickly, seeking a high return-on-effort orientation to insights. How do you implement both insight collection and quick reverse engineering? That is not the way most organizations pursue competitive intelligence.

Try this: Starting with your Big Bet Memo Experiments, focus your reverse engineering on just the killer feature and the associated key operating features. If possible, be a customer and see for yourself. From there, conduct interviews with former executives, current leaders, and key technology vendors for the company you are targeting. Ask not just about the current capability, but about their vision for new innovations, challenges, details, and ideas they are considering. Expert interview network services, from companies like GLG or Guidepoint, are marketplaces for gaining legitimate access to experts for interviews.

SYSTEMS THINKING THROUGH FLYWHEEL STRATEGIES

With this valuable information in hand, we move to the next phase of the chess match: understanding the battlefield.

Here's an example that takes us back to Bill Gates:

Gates and his then wife Melinda French Gates formed The Bill & Melinda Gates Foundation in 2000. The philanthropic efforts started as the Gates Library Foundation in 2000. In 2008, Gates transitioned out of a day-to-day role at Microsoft and focused much more of his time and energy at the Foundation.[9] The Gates Foundation, which is the world's second-largest philanthropy, states that its mission is "to create a world where every person has the opportunity to live a healthy, productive life."[10]

In the fall of 2009, spurred by the $4.35 billion Race to the Top grant program from the US Department of Education, the Gates Foundation sensed a once-in-a-generation opportunity to create change in the US education ecosystem.

The Gates Foundation team had a long-held developing strategy of trying to promote longitudinal student data to improve student experience and outcomes. Longitudinal data refers to the ability to collect many key pieces of data on individual students. Examples include campus enrollment each year; programs in which the student receives services; ethnicity; and age. John Rossman was engaged in assisting in the development of a grant strategy in response to the Race to the Top program. The situation had many actors, diverse agendas, divisions, policies, and obstacles. The current system is an example of a wicked problem.

In "Strategy as a Wicked Problem," author John Camillus outlines five characteristics of strategy-related wicked problems. First, the problem involves many stakeholders with different values and priorities. Second, the issue's roots are complex and tangled. Third, the problem is difficult to come to grips with and changes with every attempt to address it. Fourth, the challenge has no precedent. Finally, there is nothing to indicate the right answer to the problem.[11]

As the team studied the situation and the many past assessments the Foundation had developed, these conditions had all the characteristics of a wicked problem. How would we develop a meaningful understanding of the system? We developed a framework familiar to the technology world: System dynamics, causal loops, and flywheels.

A flywheel strategy is a business strategy focusing on creating a virtuous cycle of growth and momentum. The concept is based on the idea of a flywheel, which is a large, heavy wheel that takes a lot of energy to start spinning, but once it gets going, it becomes easier to keep it spinning.

Similarly, a flywheel strategy aims to create a self-sustaining cycle of growth by focusing on three key elements: attracting customers, delivering a great customer experience, and using that customer feedback to continuously improve the product or service. Amazon's flywheel model is the most famous.

By adding third-party sellers, selection increases; increasing selection improves the customer experience; when the customer experience improves, site web traffic increases; when site web traffic increases, more sellers are attracted to the platform. All of this drives a lower cost structure, which allows for prices to be lowered, feeding back into the flywheel. This drives growth.

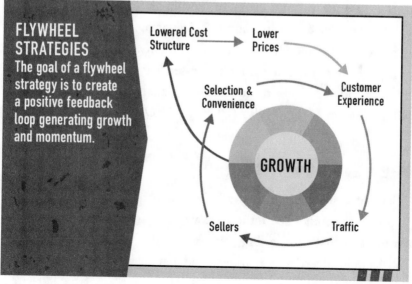

FLYWHEEL STRATEGIES
The goal of a flywheel strategy is to create a positive feedback loop generating growth and momentum.

Lowered Cost Structure → Lower Prices

Selection & Convenience

Customer Experience

GROWTH

Sellers

Traffic

This approach can be effective for companies looking to build a sustainable and scalable business model. By understanding the US educational system as a set of actors, and the creation and use of longitudinal data as the problem to solve, a system understanding of how the Gates Foundation might proceed with a set of grants was formed and effectively communicated.

Applying systems thinking and envisioning the future iteration of a complex scenario through the metaphor of a flywheel significantly enhances our comprehension. This approach not only strengthens our capacity to articulate the intricacies of the situation to ourselves and others, but also sharpens our focus on the heart of the issue and the essential outcomes needed for effective problem resolution.

THE OTHER PEOPLE'S OUTCOMES FLYWHEEL MEMO

In a novel manner, the Other People's Outcomes Memo and the flywheel design are joined into a compelling explanation of the logic, techniques, strategy, and key risks to solve the problem through the Big Bet.

From the benchmarking evaluation, identify the scenario with the most intriguing flywheel effect, which is the one causing the greatest degree of upheaval and evolution within the ecosystem. Develop a flywheel model to encapsulate this scenario. To avoid limiting the interpretation to merely visual representations, draft a supplementary two-page memo highlighting the essential insights and learnings relevant to your Thinking in Outcomes analysis. This written piece will be known as the *Big Bet Other People's Outcomes Flywheel Memo*.

THE NEXT ERA OF MICROSOFT

Microsoft's stock hit a then all-time high of $55.75 on January 7, 2000. At the end of 2013, the stock was below $40, where it had been for most of that decade. Having largely missed the mobile platform and search advertising markets, and having watched a crosstown company, Amazon—which was not considered a competitor—develop the cloud infrastructure market, was the Wintel era over and Microsoft's fortunes waning?

Satya Nadella was elevated to CEO in 2014. He began several strategy and corporate culture changes including embracing the open-source movement and a complete focus on cloud computing. But the biggest challenges were not technological changes or the US Department of Justice; they were internal challenges. Nadella has often been quoted about trying to shift Microsoft from a "know it all culture" to a "learn it all culture."[12] Microsoft stock value has increased more than fivefold since 2014, and Microsoft has been one of the few large enterprises to successfully cross technology eras.

The deliberate and paced learning focused by benchmarking analysis and conclusions is a "learn-it-all" technique applied to the mission of forming your Big Bet.

Not every flywheel results in an Amazon Marketplace, nor does reverse engineering and learning from others always result in a Microsoft Windows industry dominance. But these efforts can be critical in solving wicked problems, making better Big Bets and de-risking the situation. They help us become a "learn it all culture" and improve our understanding and proposed designs.

Problem diagnosis, customer exploration, debating, refining, clarifying, constraining, and more debating combine to create rapid and real strategy setting, experimentation, and progress.

This integrated thinking process is an adaptation of what Albert Einstein referred to as thought experiments. A thought experiment is a logical argument within the context of a hypothetical scenario. Einstein used the process to understand the revolutionary and fundamental understandings of sub-atomic physics and communicate his insights to others. Thought experiments do not report new empirical data. The idea is to stimulate one's ability to apply intuition to their understanding of a scenario and test it.

Our thought experiments, done through memos, may initially appear costly and time-consuming, but the truth is that these efforts represent the most economical and invaluable experiments that can be conducted. The approach can be likened to an archer aiming their bow. They can move the angle and direction of the bow freely before release, but once the arrow is released and in flight, the archer cannot alter its path. Similarly, we can adjust our ideas and our aim freely when in the stage of ideation and discussion. Degrees of freedom are lost early, but especially when the monthly expenses and team size increases. Once we make significant financial or market commitments to the Big Bet, we lose the ability to decide that this concept is not worth it. We have fired the arrow.

What goes along with a rapid pace of analysis, design, and testing with the Big Bet Memo Experiments? While defining clarity, maintaining velocity, and prioritizing risk and value continue to be the key habits, we need a playing field, an environment, suited for the risk and ambition of our Big Bet.

PART II

BIG BET ENVIRONMENT

"The most dangerous phrase in the language is 'we've always done it this way.'"

—GRACE HOPPER

Welcome to the Big Bet Environment, where the leaders who thrive are those who create the proper context, rules, and resources for their transformations. What are both the checklist and the equipment needed for Big Bet success in the hyper-connected, demanding, and complex company environment—an environment recognizing that the needs and mission of a Big Bet are fundamentally different from that of the existing organization? The stakes are high, and the right preparation sets the stage for clarity, velocity, and prioritization.

This "Big Bet Environment" section is organized into three chapters, each exploring a unique aspect of the environment and providing you with the tools and perspectives required to navigate it confidently.

In Chapter 3, "Opening Moves," we delve deeper into the strategic environment underpinning successful Big Bets. This chapter introduces a range of powerful strategic early moves and tactics to guide organizations toward transformative outcomes. We explore the importance of dedicated, expert, and independent teams, setting up a "get to yes" culture across the organization to support the Big Bet and avoid the hardest blockers and challenges in the Big Bet lifecycle.

Chapter 4, "Think Big, But Bet Small," introduces a core concept of *Big Bet Leadership*. It's about thinking big—daring to envision transformative outcomes for your organization—while betting small, in the sense that we work to strategically minimize the critical risks while maximizing potential rewards. This chapter connects the concepts developed in the "Big Bet Thinking" section into the environment and the further development and validation of the Big Bet.

Finally, in Chapter 5, "Championship Habits," we address a common pitfall that many leaders face when attempting to make big bets: the tendency to shrink back from their ambitious goals, settling for a more comfortable yet ultimately less rewarding middle ground. This chapter will challenge you to confront this fear and resist the temptation to play it safe. Communication and leadership culture are the change levers to keep the ambition high.

These three chapters provide a recipe for creating the Big Bet Environment—a recipe that includes the unique requirements for Big Bet success.

CHAPTER 3
OPENING MOVES

"The greatest victory is that which requires no battle."

—SUN TZU

The chess world employs tactics and moves called gambits for a particular type of early move sequences. It's typically the sacrifice of a pawn to gain a later advantage in the game.

For Big Bets, there are gambits to be made—counter-traditional opening moves that might appear to be unnecessary, wasteful, counter-policy, not what you would learn in an MBA program. We are making early, strategic moves, with the goal of securing advantages later down the road. The opening moves entail action now, with the payoff coming later. It is a mindset demanding savvy precision, intelligence, budget, and a new way of thinking.

In many ways, Big Bets are the embrace of struggle. The struggle in business is, hopefully, a never-ending journey. The struggle for growth. The struggle to differentiate. The struggle for profitability. The struggle to create a virtuous cycle instead of a vicious cycle. The struggle to recruit, grow, and retain great talent and culture. None of this is easy. All of it is necessary.

Amazon frames this struggle as a mission to stay a Day 1 company. The concept of a Day 1 company is both a leadership approach and operating model prioritizing curiosity, the willingness to experiment and fail, and removing customer friction—all while taking a customer-first mindset. A Day 1 company operates as though its best days are ahead, and thus is willing to invest a higher ratio of today's operating profits into building the future, as opposed to being a company that is trying to optimize today's short-term profits and thus does not invest in reinvention. The latter is a Day 2 company.

A Day 2 company is the subtle but distinct opposite of Day 1. A Day 2 company prioritizes short-term profitability over long-term strategy and differentiation. Day 2 leaders don't understand or embrace the inherent failure-driven nature of innovation and bets, creating a low tolerance for experimentation and risks. This is why so many great operating companies struggle with innovation, digital transformation, and other types of Big Bets. They apply the same mental framework of "operating precision" and a low tolerance for failure, which works in well-understood operations and business models, but not in the discipline of innovation, which inherently and by necessity is a trial-and-error process.

Thinking in Outcomes sets us up to understand the distinct and different game we want to be playing in the near future. And while this game has failures, our approach minimizes the risks of large failure, increases the rate of learning, and accelerates and maximizes the value of future outcomes, which will be loved by customers.

With the end outcome and key operating capabilities well defined and tested in our memo experiments, we are eager to start further development and validation. Slow down for just a second. What's missing? The key environment in which to build and test our Big Bet concepts.

In this chapter we outline key supporting leadership moves, tactics, and team formation strategies enabling Big Bet success. These are counterintuitive shortcuts and catalysts creating accelerants and risk avoidance in our Big Bet journey. But they may pose a big challenge to traditional thinking.

A team is required for your Big Bet, but that is just the obvious need. We need to establish a culture, the key processes, the policies, partnerships, technology environments, and the incentives to rapidly prove, or disprove, the Big Bet. Many of the considerations proposed here might be mischaracterized as reckless or wasteful. As we demonstrate, the truth is quite the opposite. Although one might argue that this behavior will waste a nickel, we demonstrate that these techniques create or save big dollars.

BEWARE THE LAB

One consistent topic in innovation and digital transformation discussions is how to organize. Many large enterprises have created separate digital lab organizations. Often, these are far away from the corporate center. They are rationalized as a way to access the design and technology talent the organization can't hire. Walmart Labs, GE Digital, and Ford's Silicon Valley lab were all based in the northern California Silicon Valley area. The idea was to locate in the center of digital innovation and thereby achieve the same results as other Silicon Valley companies. The efforts were expensive and the results decidedly mixed.

So, what happened? Not enough free kombucha and yoga breaks? Maybe. But the real reason these bets did not pay out goes to the setup of the environment. Our experience in creating teams, leadership, and environments to succeed at Big Bets such as digital transformations and innovation programs is this: Bring constraints and expectations of results to the team. Avoid the science fair syndrome, which has beleaguered so many innovation programs. Placing constraints on the team works, but it comes with requirements and costs. It demands that an independent environment be created. In this alternate universe, everything is optimized for speed—speed to decisions, speed to prototypes, speed to learning, and speed to adjustments.

We generally support having separate teams to drive Big Bets because of the skills, focus, and complexity of the mission required for Big Bets. We are skeptical of creating these teams without constraints, ties, and a well-defined mission to create a sense of urgency and agency. Expectations must be present, no matter where your Big Bet team is located. It's not about a place on the map; it's all about the environment you create.

Let's discuss the essential elements of the environment.

BUILDING A TEAM, THE HOLLYWOOD WAY

Big Bet experimenting is a lot like developing a movie script. We are writing and producing a story with the Big Bet Memo Experiments, with the future customer experience and business concept in mind. Now we need to bring it to life, developing a prototype of the movie to see if we have nailed it. Will the story resonate with the audience?

To build the story and prototypes, we need a movie production studio and a specialized team.

Movies are produced with a team that is funded and supervised by a studio organization. But the team is a healthy mix of company employees and outside contractors. This team comes together for a purpose. It is a carefully chosen group of professionals, all with key skills and armed with a willingness to become obsessed with this future blockbuster we are calling our Big Bet. The team is optimized for skills, focus, expertise, and output—not longevity.

This team differs decidedly from the traditional enterprise project or operations. How do ordinary enterprise leaders lead programs? The person in charge, in addition to having their regular operational role, goes begging for participation from other teams for the skills required. "I need a development team"; "I need marketing input"; "I need legal participation"; "I need expertise on any number of topics."

What this leader receives in return is a commitment of a share of many people's bandwidth to support the work alongside those individuals' broader project portfolios and day-to-day responsibilities.

This fractional team is more than just fractional time; it means fractional ownership, fractional accountability, and fractional thinking. They are not obsessed. Typical and well-understood projects might lend themselves to being executed in this manner, but vital and risky endeavors cannot. Not Big Bets.

A Big Bet needs a dedicated team. Coupled with Thinking in Outcomes, having a full-time team is perhaps the single most important controllable factor in winning Big Bets. Focus, ownership, skills, critical thinking, and commitment are all required. A dedicated core team is part of the Big Bet Vector.

Amazon's version of this principle is a Two-Pizza Team. A team of five to ten people, which typically could be fed by two pizzas, is given the mission of obsessing over, building, and operating a capability. Giving a team a clearly defined mission via the Thinking in Outcomes Memos with the mandate and ability to focus, to obsess, to build, to test, and to solve wicked problems is vital.

A team requires a captain—someone intellectually, tactically, and emotionally leading the charge. Could one reasonably expect a general manager to allocate 20 percent of their time to this Big Bet and achieve success? It doesn't work.

Big Bets require a core full-time team led by a full-time senior person. Hard stop. This committed leader concept is not new. Apple and others in Silicon Valley have named it—a directly responsible individual (DRI).[1] A directly responsible individual is a senior person fully responsible for the Big Bet. "A common phrase heard around Apple when someone is trying to learn the right contact on a project [is] 'Who's the DRI on that?'"[2]

Amazon has essentially the same leadership approach on hard or new initiatives: the single-threaded leader. The single-threaded leader is singularly and fully focused on leading a complex initiative and is not affected by competing responsibilities. Dave Limp, the former Senior Vice President of Devices and Services at Amazon, said it this way: "The best way to fail at inventing something is by making it somebody's part-time job."[3] At Amazon, once a proposal gets an okay to proceed, a leader is assigned to it. It may or may not be the person who first proposed the idea or the development of the initial memos. "We empower the single-threaded leader to go off and make great things."

Clearly, the term "single-threaded leader" is a nod to programming and means that the leader isn't expected to multitask. As Jeff Wilke, the former CEO of Amazon's Worldwide Consumer Business stated, this is "someone who wakes up and just worries about that thing." That's "super important to how we invent."[4]

It's required that this individual is senior enough to be given decision-making authority, probably more authority than you are used to giving. This leader must influence and negotiate with other senior leaders and partners on behalf of the initiative. They need to be a talent magnet and understand that building a great team and culture quickly, both internally and externally, is a critical part of the job.

In some cases, consider a two-in-a-box leadership model. Consider pairing the Big Bet leader with an external interim leader who has experience in the domains, risks, and team management defined by our Big Bet. Perhaps this person brings significant experience in large platform migrations or in artificial intelligence. Having this person tagged as "interim" helps bring independence and external experiences to the leadership team. It mitigates the inherent risk of a single-threaded leader—which is the fact that they are single-threaded. Having redundancy at the initiative leadership level is a small insurance policy against the Big Bet leader not being available either short-term, for example for vacations, or long-term, perhaps leaving for another job.

This interim operator is a special breed of leader. They operate in duality, understanding they are a decision-maker and hands-on leader, while also sometimes acting as an advisor and facilitator.

Building the right team, including leadership, often requires a true gambit—the need to sacrifice some degree of speed of execution to get the decisions right in anticipation of long-term benefits. It is always tempting to build a team and assign leadership based on availability so as to get going quickly, but the time saved by staffing a Big

Bet with the most available talent instead of the most qualified will be lost ten times over further down the road.

ESTABLISH EXPERT PARTNERS, NOT GATEKEEPERS

There are key Big Bet supporting functions and stakeholders, but they might not be needed full-time. These functions might include legal, human resources, IT, tax, or manufacturing, among others.

A key rule of the Big Bet game: Whenever there are stakeholders who have control over the velocity of the Big Bet, they need to be a part of the team. If the legal function can create a hard stop, they are part of the team. Supply chain plays a role in a key operational capability? You're in the band.

These stakeholders don't need to be dedicated to the initiative, but they do need the mindset that supporting the success of the Big Bet is their primary objective. This is not typical in most enterprises, where the primary drivers would be the typical run-the-business policies, pace, and constraints of the function, with a secondary goal of supporting the success of the Big Bet.

What mindset do these critical partners need?

Traditional organizations often have a core team running a specific project, with functional teams like finance, legal, and HR offering support. Unfortunately, these support teams are sometimes seen as "specialists" whose role is narrowly defined. They may be viewed as obstacles rather than collaborators, often providing reasons why something can't be done or outlining strict requirements to achieve a goal.

Remember those moments when internal negotiations felt tougher than the project itself? In some cases, the legal team could have been dubbed the "deal prevention squad" because their safest bet against risk was to say "no." This leads to a culture in which the easiest answer is to decline rather than explore possibilities.

However, for successful big bets, we need a shift in culture, especially from these critical support partners. Instead of pointing out why something won't work, the focus should be on relevant questions: How can we make it work? What options do we have? What are the potential trade-offs and opportunities? Getting to a "yes" should be the collective goal of the entire team, not just the core business team. Even when faced with difficult challenges, no one should just walk away. In this new culture, everyone shares the responsibility and ownership of finding that "yes," making the journey toward it a collaborative effort.

CULTIVATE PARTNERS, NOT VENDORS

When the stakes are high, you need the tools to win. Specialized skills are often needed. And the people with these specialized skills need the most valuable asset of all—availability. These are contractors and consultants with expertise, outside-in perspectives, and an undistracted full-time obsession for your Big Bet.

But only if you really want to win.

There are several talent agencies, such as a-connect and Catalant, offering low-friction access to a marketplace of specialized independent consulting and technical talent.

That kind of team is built quickly, needs to be focused, and often has a standard way of working. It's likely that the team members are not needed long-term. By utilizing vendor and consulting teams in this targeted and strategic manner, we minimize the impact on existing jobs and sacrifice neither velocity nor expertise. This is often the time to have consulting and technical development teams and contractors involved. This is not at the exclusion of employees and hiring for this team, but having access to talent that is focused on speed and deployment flexibility.

Develop a consistent set of relationships and options so tapping contractor resources is seamless. Here's the leadership mindset mistake many organizations make at this juncture: They create a win-lose mentality with their partners, making it into a vendor relationship versus a partner relationship. Get the best out of your partners by always encouraging frank and problem-first communications.

POLICIES AND PROCEDURES

Policies and procedures play a pivotal role in expediting success within high-expectation environments that demand specialized expertise. Consider the predicament of a world-class downhill skier asked to win a race using cross-country skis; victory is improbable. Likewise, a dedicated team tackling a wicked problem must be equipped with the proper policies and decision-making autonomy to prevail.

To win Big Bets, it's essential to recognize that traditional policies may hinder progress rather than support it. Reevaluating such policies can help minimize friction and maximize the local accountability necessary to achieve ambitious goals, enabling the team to overcome even the most daunting challenges.

Traditional procurement practices often prioritize a win-lose mindset, focused solely on optimizing the price per unit purchased. While this approach works well for established, operational businesses, it's not ideal for ambitious, high-stake initiatives—the Big Bets.

For Big Bets, we're not looking for the cheapest option but for the right blend of expertise and capabilities to tackle the toughest challenges swiftly and flexibly. This requires a shift from conventional procurement thinking. It's crucial that we adjust our approach to align with the mission, and not let minor priorities unintentionally overshadow our main objectives.

Existing policies—be they hiring, procurement, or IT—that were designed for standard operations need to be reevaluated and tweaked to support the Big Bet's mission. This might involve altering vendor approval lists, project approval processes, and specific IT or procurement policies.

But how can you bring about these changes while leading a Big Bet? You don't have the luxury to overhaul backend processes across the organization. The solution is to involve leaders and stakeholders from partner organizations in your team. Give them the context of the Big Bet and encourage them to adjust their policies to better serve the needs of the Big Bet. Ensure consistent, early communication about specific areas that need to be addressed, instilling a "get to yes" culture. It's about making these individuals stakeholders in the success of the Big Bet, giving them a reason to adapt and support your mission.

YOUR OWN PRIVATE DIGITAL IDAHO

The corporate IT department, with its legacy technology and data environments, more than likely poses the greatest tactical challenge for organizations attempting to follow the *Big Bet Leadership* playbook.

The corporate IT team find themselves in a difficult position. They are expected to drive innovation and disruptive technology while simultaneously maintaining stability and ensuring smooth operations. Balancing these demands is a tall order, and there is often little room for ambitious, forward-thinking projects where business cases are still being proven.

The *Big Bet Leadership* playbook wants to pull testing of the largest risks forward and defer the major expense and long development cycles. The classic large technology platform roadmap does the exact opposite.

So, what's the solution?

Waiting for the IT organization's platform transformation to solve the problem isn't advisable. Alternatively, postponing the issue until you're ready to scale your big bet is a risky move. It may result in derailing your project at a critical moment, giving competitors the chance to capitalize on your efforts. Instead, it's essential to address any IT dependencies up front and develop strategies to mitigate potential threats.

One creative approach is to establish an "alternate universe," a separate environment where you can rapidly prototype, experiment, and test new integrations and solutions without the constraints of a traditional IT operating model. Inspired by the concept of a digital twin, this environment mimics key data, schematics, and rules from the legacy system but is designed for rapid innovation, simulations, and testing.

To create your alternate universe, consider the following strategies:

First, develop an isolated technology stack that includes the essential components for testing and prototyping, such as CRM, order management, and supply chain systems. Aim for a pre-integrated stack from a single vendor and ensure compatibility with cutting-edge technologies, such as AI and machine learning.

Second, partner with innovative technology providers, such as Palantir, that offer rapid implementation and disruptive solutions. With proprietary technology for software-defined data integration and AI environments spanning multiple disparate data silos—technology that brings together the disjointed data and schematics across the organization—Palantir routinely provides simulation environments with full-scale data, analytics, and business operations in weeks, not months.

Once in place, environments such as this might be able to play an even bigger role: helping to avoid Big Bet technology migrations. An example of Palantir providing rapid results by adding a system of intelligence layer over a varied technology landscape is found in the company's work at Panasonic Energy Corporation. "This strategic partnership is intended to provide the battery leader with the ability to quickly generate meaningful cost savings and increase return on investment once implemented."[5] This implementation took weeks, not a year or more, to assimilate the data from a complex and disparate environment.

Third, utilize low-code tools to create front-end, mobile applications and AI models while integrating to disruptive technologies and data sets, creating prototypes for validation in days and weeks, not months. Engaging an expert developer as part of your team allows you to utilize these tools with speed and avoid potential pitfalls, and again, increases speed to testing, learning, and validation.

Low-code environments for developing AI-driven applications offer significant advantages in terms of speed and productivity. These platforms provide visual development tools, reusable components, and pre-built templates, enabling developers to create applications faster and more efficiently, even with limited coding experience. Productivity improvements typically range from 50 percent to 90 percent, depending on the project and the developers' expertise. The benefits include faster time-to-market, reduced development costs, easier integration with AI services and APIs, and simplified maintenance.

By creating an alternate universe, dependencies on legacy systems and the teams supporting them are minimized. While not relevant for every Big Bet, investing in your alternate universe is an investment that—like building a dedicated high-performing team—has an incredible ROI.

INCENTIVES

To ignore incentives would be to ignore basic human behavior. Incentives need to be strategically considered, not just for the team on the Big Bet, but for key partners and the entire executive team.

For the Big Bet team leader, the DRI, and the core team, think through the career path. Ensure that "testing the Big Bet, iterating a good one, and avoiding a bad Big Bet" is a great outcome for team members. Access to and mentorship from the CEO help incentivize and groom great talent.

For Big Bet team members, including partners, incentivize for the outcomes the team is optimizing for: speed to learnings and proving out the critical risks of a winning value proposition. Operate in true sprints. Sprint; take a rest. Sprint; take a rest. Cash bonuses or other rewards are appropriate for demo proof points and finishing the test cycles. These don't need to be substantial, just a token of recognition.

Gain executive alignment to the Big Bet. Even the nature of incentive programs for executives may have to be redesigned, because a company is now using different metrics for success. Robert Iger, CEO of The Walt Disney Company, disclosed that executive stock grants for some Disney employees would be determined by how much they contribute to the implementation of the strategy driving the launch of Disney Plus. Now, Disney is making stock grants "that would vest or mature based on my own assessment of whether executives were stepping up to make this new initiative successful," Iger wrote.[6]

But don't forget that the No. 1 incentive is removing the disincentives. This is the bureaucracy, and the slow-moving rules that apply to the scaled business. The people attracted to leading these teams are looking for speed of decision-making, which they realize is the biggest challenge in driving Big Bets. As Paul Graham of Y Combinator says, "startups die of suicide, not homicide."[7] This saying applies to all companies, programs, digital transformations, strategy development, mergers, innovation initiatives, and all our Big Bets. We typically beat ourselves through a lack of alignment and by not addressing the true disincentives and not enabling the team through the best environment to succeed.

OPTIMIZING THROUGH ISOLATION

We have tackled team leadership, team composition, managing key stakeholders, culture, policies, minimizing dependencies such as technology, and creating incentives for those involved. All of this is an effort to optimize for the three habits of Big Bet legends:

First, creating clarity—a dedicated team focused on a defined and ambitious Big Bet.

Second, maintaining velocity—a pace of decision making and progress different from the one at which the organization typically operates.

Third, prioritizing risk and value—maintaining scope and attention to high-value, high-risk elements for validation.

Combined with Big Bet Thinking, the Big Bet Vector is set.

THE OPENING MOVES ARE COMPLETE

The success of Big Bets depends on optimizing team leadership, composition, focus, stakeholder management, culture, and policies;

minimizing dependencies; and incentivizing key players. By focusing on these aspects, organizations create an environment fostering accountability, urgency, and innovation, while avoiding the bureaucratic pitfalls that often derail ambitious projects.

To optimize for speed and focus, organizations must address potential dependencies such as technology and procurement policies, establish the alternate universe for rapid prototyping and testing, and create tailored incentive structures for Big Bet team members and executives. By tackling these challenges head-on and fostering an environment purpose-built for the Big Bet, organizations can significantly increase the likelihood of success for their Big Bets and drive meaningful outcomes.

Even a company like Google suffers from an inability to innovate and create an environment conducive to successful Big Bets. A senior product leader who left Google in 2023 said that employees are "'trapped in a maze of approvals, launch processes, legal reviews, performance reviews, exec reviews, documents, meetings, bug reports, triage, OKRs, H1 plans followed by H2 plans, all-hands summits, and inevitable reorgs.' So much so that they 'get very little done quarter over quarter, year over year.'"[8]

If Google is unable to overcome these dynamics—each of which is a barrier to both focus and speed, or a clear vector—it is highly likely that Google will be watching from the sidelines as others capture Big Bet opportunities right in Google's own backyard. Every company should explicitly evaluate the opening moves that would be key in creating an environment for successful transformations.

In the next chapter, we put these opening moves to use by not confusing "thinking big" with "betting big."

CHAPTER 4

THINK BIG, BUT BET SMALL

"The greater danger for most of us lies not in setting our aim too high and falling short, but in setting our aim too low and achieving our mark."

—MICHELANGELO

The typical transformation, enterprise strategy, or major technology initiative has a methodical, left-to-right and build-from-the-foundation-up mindset. These methodologies might be appropriate for well understood, low-risk programs, like a finance system implementation or building a new transportation network. The primary risk in these investments is execution risk; thus, proceeding in the structured model is appropriate.

Even in innovation programs or environments where the Agile methodology is used, it is often within a framework of plan, commit, build, get results. Perhaps the details of the user interface and technology components are done in sprints and with the goal of trying to ship product weekly, but the sequence of what is being built is still led with the left-to-right, bottom-to-top mindset.

Get ready to flip the script and prioritize differently.

In a revealing interview with the noted internet investor turned journalist Henry Blodgett, Jeff Bezos gave a master class in experimentation and innovation for other leaders. At first glance, a short statement by Bezos catches our attention: "I don't believe in bet-the-company bets."[1]

Wait.

What?

Jeff Bezos doesn't believe in Big Bets?

Of course, he does. Read the entire section. "Companies that don't continue to experiment, companies that don't embrace failure, they eventually get in a desperate position where the only thing they can do is a Hail Mary bet at the very end of their corporate existence. Whereas companies that are making bets all along, even big bets, but not bet-the-company bets, prevail. I don't believe in bet-the-company bets. That's when you're desperate. That's the last thing you can do."[2]

What Bezos rejects is a particular kind of Big Bet—one that often goes disastrously wrong. These are Bet-the-Company Bets. Often these types of bets are forced upon a leadership team because they have run out of options, have not been investing in the future of their business, and have to place significant, catch-up and turn-around style moves.

In this chapter, we dive into the concept Bezos understood so well. The best kind of Big Bet is one that avoids potential catastrophic risk by accelerating testing and validation of the critical risks and deferring major commitments. Successful users of this strategy know that there's a time and a place for investing big. And it's not at the starting gate.

DON'T BET THE RANCH

People often cite Bezos' admission that he made billions of dollars' worth of failures en route to Amazon's successes as proof that companies need to be willing to take big swings to capture big opportunities. Over the last two decades, we have witnessed company executives championing that the moment for the major transformation is here and big commitments are needed. "We must" the executive says, "commit to several hundred million dollars over the next two years to capture this multi-billion-dollar opportunity! It's what Bezos would do!"

Except it's not. That is not at all what Bezos would do. That is not, in fact, what he actually did. Instead, Amazon developed a playbook for taking ideas from concept to scale aggressively but efficiently. "If you invent frequently and are willing to fail, then you never get to the point where you really need to bet the whole company," according to Bezos.[3] The key to that playbook is a mindset followed by an action. The key is to think big, but bet small.

The launch of Amazon's Marketplace business in 2002 was a Big Bet. It paid off. This business supports millions of sellers and is responsible for close to 60 percent of all units shipped and sold at Amazon. Developing a big vision for creating an outstanding customer and seller experience was critical in laying the foundation for success. Amazon Web Services (AWS), Kindle, Prime—all of Amazon's proven Big Bets started as relatively modest investments, but with a big vision.

Let us bring you into the story of the Amazon Marketplace as an example. As the big vision and strategy for the marketplace business emerged, two core principles were deemed critical to success:

The first is *trust*. Customers should trust buying from a third party as much as they trust buying from Amazon, the first-party retailer. To realize this, the entire customer experience with third-party sellers needed to be indistinguishable from the experience of buying directly from Amazon. Leading with the Amazon concept of "customer obsession" meant that even though Amazon was neither the seller of record nor responsible for fulfillment on the Marketplace orders, the Marketplace team operated with sellers in a partnership mindset. This principle led to a robust and complex choreography of integration points, requirements, and necessary coordination.

The second is *scale*. The team knew Marketplace needed to be able to operate a large business with low headcount and capital. The critical strategy for this was seller self-service. The Marketplace team needed to envision supporting hundreds of thousands of sellers, not hundreds of sellers. And the self-service feature was nonnegotiable. Marketplace established early partners and built technology helping sellers integrate, test, and operate. An extensive roadmap of capabilities for scaling while enabling trust was established.

There was tension between these two principles. Creating trust meant tight integration, control, and oversight with sellers. This strategy was completely different from that of eBay, the dominant marketplace in 2002. eBay had more of a Wild West aura to its operations.

But for the Amazon Marketplace to scale meant making it easy for sellers and for Amazon to have a lean cost structure in the Marketplace seller operations. The Amazon flywheel required tens of thousands of sellers and millions of new items, growing later to millions of sellers and hundreds of millions of items. It was the combination of these two principles that forced better design, creativity, and innovations. Constraints and opposing goals forced better thinking.

These principles were the high-level outcomes envisioned in the Marketplace business. They were also unproven concepts. The team didn't know if customers would adopt the offering. Frankly, there were internal doubts, internal naysayers, as to whether sellers could operate with the precision Amazon displayed and demanded. Plenty of Amazon's senior fulfillment and operations leaders believed that these sellers could not deliver to meet the Amazon customer service promise. The Marketplace was a leap. Could sellers achieve both customer trust and scale-through to self-service with Amazon-worthy speed and operational precision?

This Big Bet was framed as building a multi-category retail marketplace with authoritative selection, a high-trust customer experience, and a truly scalable operational business model. But Amazon didn't make that full jump right away. Before there could be a Big Bet, there needed to be first bets.

The Marketplace wasn't going to be built in one release. Although at the time Amazon didn't have the vernacular of Agile methodology, minimum viable product, or objectives and key results (OKRs), this was how the team was acting. Amazon thought in terms of outcomes, constraints, and fast feedback.

Defining outcomes and constraints allows you to avoid analysis paralysis and overbuilding. They prevent scope creep. When you have scope creep, you must invest more to support that larger project, and progress slows. And then you invest more. And more. And more. Eventually you can't afford to let it fail, even if it should. Outcomes and constraints prevent thinking big from inadvertently turning into betting big—overinvesting prior to critical learning. Instead, fine tuning and proof points are developed. It's not always fun to go through that learning process. In Amazon's case, the key and difficult first outcomes were:

- Launch the apparel category in time for the holiday season of 2002.

- Launch with all key apparel partners—about forty in total.

- Enable "size" and "color" variations on a single detail page, which was a major new feature for Amazon, having significant technology impact.

- Provide an integrated shopping cart, checkout, and single payment experience—also a brand-new set of features. Again, a major technology re-architecture.

  Everything else the team faked, hustled, postponed, delayed, and compensated for with unscalable human effort. This was intentional and designed as a short-term arrangement.

Post-launch, Amazon began adding key elements, including:

- Creating a self-service registration pipeline. This enabled sellers to register. Once the data was collected by the seller, all Amazon systems and credentials were updated.

- Creating a test environment and automated test criteria approach. In this system, sellers could validate that their data and choreography was correct. This was actually difficult to test end-to-end, including payments and orders.

- Creating "item authority" by reconciling items being sold by multiple sellers. If more than one merchant wanted to sell the same item, item authority determined the best content and representation for that item and reconciled the data for the accepted version of the item. This is what customers saw on the Amazon detail page. Many sellers could offer to sell that item.

- Building a partner network assisting sellers who lacked key capabilities. The data integration and processing requirements were sophisticated. Professional services, expertise, and software tools assisted merchants with this hard systems integration work.

- Creating different paths and methods of integrating to suit merchant preferences. Some sellers preferred to integrate via an API sending XML data; some sellers preferred sending a flat file of data via an API; some sellers preferred doing a manual upload of the bulk data to a website; some sellers preferred to use purely online tools and forms to build their item catalog one by one and to manually receive and process their orders. Amazon made it work for all of them.

- Building a seller-tools team. This was the product team building many of the core technologies to improve the seller experience or build operations teams' technology to assist in managing a large number of sellers.

Amazon was thinking big. But it was not confusing thinking big with betting big. Amazon envisioned the outcomes and core components of the Marketplace business at the start. The team sequenced them, launched them, and proved the risky hypotheses. It kept iterating, improving, and then committed as risks were resolved.

The constraints and top-down attention to detail forced a decision-making and delivery pace enabled with clear eyes and no confusion about the decision-making. It only took a handful of leaders—a core leadership team of about seven. The team made 95 percent of all decisions and worked on the same floor in proximity. This came in handy when Bezos would cruise by on his Segway scooter.

Before Rossman even joined the Marketplace team in early 2002, Amazon had already tried—and failed—to build two other third-party seller models. Before Amazon Marketplace, there was Amazon Auctions and then zShops. The first two were failures; the third, the current Marketplace, became the "dreamy business" Bezos referred to in the 2015 Amazon shareholder letter. Dreamy businesses display four key characteristics, Bezos said: Customers love it, it can grow to very large size, it has strong returns on capital, and it's durable in time.[4]

Bezos was committed to realizing the vision for the dreamy business that became the Marketplace as Amazon continued to bet on the strategy but adjusted the tactics and model to accomplish it. One might be tempted to imagine that at some point in 2002 Rossman had a meeting with Bezos and the S-Team that ended with Amazon's commitment to invest hundreds of millions of dollars in try number three to make sure they finally got it right.

But that didn't happen.

Not only was 2002 a scrappy year for the small Marketplace team; so were 2003 and 2004. It wasn't for several more years that Marketplace proved itself enough that the business began to see that kind of investment. We have routinely witnessed executive leaders request high levels of funding immediately following the conclusion of a strategy and planning exercise. And that's a recipe for failure. It's betting too much, too early, and invites in several risks and traditional approaches.

Both of us have seen this happen. McCaffrey witnessed a senior executive at a Fortune 100 company convince the executive team and board to "bet big" on organically building a new business line. It was in a space that had been proven by start-ups that lacked the mature and scaled go-to-market resources of a big firm. The senior exec called the opportunity "highly perishable" and a "foundational investment."

Fast-forward two years and that Fortune 100 launched its first live product to customers after $120 million of direct investment.

Contrast that with the leading start-up in the space that had spent a total of about $5 million in seed funding to generate its first $10 million of revenues. Fast-forward another three years and the start-up had added nearly $2 billion to its valuation. Meanwhile, after crippling early customer feedback, the Fortune 100 company shut down its new product line without having generated any revenue. What happened? A premature Big Bet was placed before solving away the biggest risks.

PUTTING THE MENTALITY INTO ACTION

There are many well-known and well-defined manners and resources for testing business concepts. The *Testing Business Ideas* book in the Strategyzer book series is one.[5] An example testing technique is called the "Wizard of Oz" approach, in which a capability appears to be automated or fully developed, but in fact, just as for the Wizard behind the curtain, humans are doing the task by hand.

There are dozens of frameworks, methodologies, and aids for testing concepts—all are very helpful, with *Agile* being one of the most common. *Agile* as a methodology is intended to be an approach for iterative, incremental solution design and delivery. Who wouldn't want to be agile?

Well-implemented Agile approaches and cultures are rare. Often, we've seen Agile implementation become the methodology of no accountability. *Scope, time, cost? You can't hold us accountable because we are agile (wink, wink). We are testing and learning and that's all that matters!* Teams become wholly noncommittal to outcomes or constraints. They lose a sense of urgency and accountability. They become enamored with the techniques, instead of oriented with a sense of urgency to deliver the right meaningful results. The semantic travesty occurs when *agile* is used as an excuse for not getting *real* outcomes.

Here's what we suggest instead.

THE BIG BET EXPERIMENT PLANNER

The job to be done by the Big Bet Experiment Planner is to push the main sources of risk into the daylight. Put them front and center in a clearly communicated format for everyone to see and obsess over. This is the Big Bet Leadership innovation to prioritize value and risk—one of the Big Bet Legends' critical habits.

The Big Bet Experiment Planner includes a stack-ranked list of the most important beliefs, or hypotheses, that, if true, eliminate the risks, greatly improving the odds of success for the Big Bet. How are these hypotheses surfaced? The good news is that by Thinking in Outcomes, they are already known. The exercise is deliberately simple—just refer to the Big Bet Memo Experiments:

- The What Sucks Memo
- The Outcome Definition Memo
- The Outcome Financial Memo
- The Other People's Outcomes Memo
- The Other People's Outcomes Flywheel Memo

Revisit each of these and ask, "What are the key beliefs that must be true for this Big Bet to work?" Consolidate the answers into a single list and then stack-rank the hypotheses. For each hypothesis, ask "How much more confident would I be about the likelihood of success if the hypothesis is true?" If the answer is "A lot!" put that hypothesis at the top of the list. If the answer is "A little," put it at the bottom of the list.

Be careful to avoid overcomplicating this stack-ranking exercise. After all, each hypothesis matters, or it wouldn't be on the list in the first place. The goal in stack-ranking is to ensure that high-value risks rise to the top. When it comes to prioritization exercises, teams often get bogged down in analysis paralysis by overengineering scoring rubrics. The important approach here is to create crystal clarity around the hypotheses counted on for success, and their relative importance.

Once that is done, follow this process to confirm your first pass ranking:

If hypotheses that prove a distinctive customer value proposition and scalable economics are not in the top five, reconsider. This is valid even for internal initiatives in which the customer is an employee of the company (i.e., an internal user).

For each hypothesis, ask "If this Big Bet were to quickly take off, how confident am I that we could solve the challenge underlying this hypothesis?" If the answer is "Not at all confident. I'd be really scared to see the Big Bet begin to scale before building more confidence around this hypothesis," this hypothesis goes to the top of the list! That's a high-value and high-risk hypothesis. It needs your attention. If the answer is "I'm not too sure how we'd address this challenge, but I am fully confident we'd figure it out," it goes to the lower half of the list. It's not a critical risk. You can get to it later.

That might sound obvious, but it's surprising how often teams focus early efforts and significant resources on validating what are truly high-value but low-risk hypotheses.

In one example we witnessed, a company working to launch a new product line invested 80% of early-stage resourcing into building out customer billing systems. That is a clear violation of the "think big but bet small" guideline of deprioritizing challenges that you are confident you would be able to solve if significant demand materializes. Billing systems are hard, but are not a conceptual high-risk item—billing systems do exist.

Meanwhile, the team deprioritized validating the customer value proposition and unit cost risks. The result? The company has a modern billing system for a product that few customers want to buy. The wrong risks were prioritized and resourced.

DESIGNING EXPERIMENTS

Continue to leverage and extend the Big Bet Experiment Planner. Add in experiment options and finding the fastest but still valid approach to testing. Each experiment is designed to create feedback via a prototype, proof point, research, or other technique. We are looking for a high ROE—which could stand for "Return on Experimentation" or "Return on Effort." The experiment needs to effectively prove or disprove a hypothesis. When a single experiment can help prove multiple hypotheses, great! That's a feature of the experiment, not a bug.

The Big Bet Experiment Planner ends up as a backlog, or a prioritized list of experiments. When building, the goal is not to create detailed workplans and budgets for each experiment. This takes too long and creates false precision. Instead, capture the most pertinent information to decide which experiments to activate first. The Lean Startup and Agile methodologies are great inspiration for how to do this well. For each experiment, we suggest capturing the following information:

Short Description: Between three and five sentences explaining the test or prototype to be created.

Hypotheses addressed: Cross-reference the prioritized list of hypotheses addressed by the experiment. It might be more than one hypothesis. Note the rank of each hypothesis from your stack-ranked list.

Potential for eliminating ambiguity: This is a qualitative assessment intended to help the team eliminate as much ambiguity as possible, as fast as possible. Each hypothesis on the stack rank list is surrounded by a certain amount of ambiguity, or uncertainty about how the future will unfold. The aim here is to qualitatively indicate how much of that ambiguity could be eliminated by conducting the experiment being considered. Don't over-engineer this. Use the "T-shirt sizing" approach common in Agile methodologies. If you believe that successfully conducting the experiment would fully address the doubts surrounding a target hypothesis, assign an XL T-shirt size. If you believe that the results would be informative, but a significant number of additional experiments would be required to fully eliminate doubts, assign an XS T-shirt size.

Investment: Frame this as a percentage of the total resources, factoring both monetary and team effort, available for the current phase of your Big Bet. Again, don't over-engineer this.

Scope each experiment such that the result can be demonstrated within three months or faster. Repeat—all experiments must be completed and have demonstrated results in three months or less. This constraint becomes important in building an efficient operating rhythm and in forcing prioritization for the Big Bet.

TRANSITION TO SEQUENCING

With the Big Bets Experiments Planner in hand, it is again time to prioritize. Choose which experiments to run first. To do this, employ a version of the "weighted shortest job first" approach recommended in Agile methodologies. This prioritization technique is a way to rationalize and optimize value delivery by assigning a priority to various units of work—in this case, the experiments in the experiments backlog.

Once again, do not overcomplicate this! If your organization is an agile machine, well accustomed to sprint planning sessions, it is fine to employ a more rigorous approach. However, in our experience, prioritization approaches that often masquerade as rigorous are in fact simply suffering from false precision. A strong Big Bet team can simplify and accelerate by collaboratively sequencing the experiments in the experiments backlog with a focus on prioritizing experiments that perform well on the three most relevant dimensions:

1. Targeting high value—in other words, top of the list—hypotheses.

2. Eliminating significant ambiguity.

3. Consuming as little investment as possible.

The team may decide to visualize the data through two-by-two's and other mechanisms. The team may choose to calculate ratios; for example, dividing a value score by an investment score. These activities are fine as long as the team spends little time on them and the results are taken with a grain of salt. The reality is that prioritizing the team's work is a top responsibility of the Big Bet DRI, and there's no substitute for business intuition.

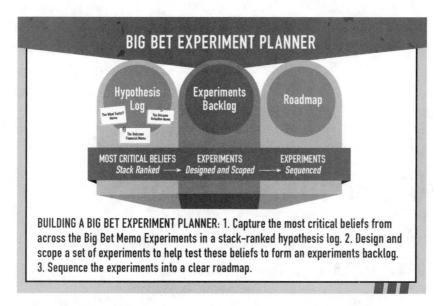

BIG BET EXPERIMENT PLANNER

Hypothesis Log
The What Tanks? Memo
The Outcome Definition Memo
The Outcome Financial Memo

Experiments Backlog

Roadmap

MOST CRITICAL BELIEFS
Stack Ranked ⟶

EXPERIMENTS
Designed and Scoped ⟶

EXPERIMENTS
Sequenced

BUILDING A BIG BET EXPERIMENT PLANNER: 1. Capture the most critical beliefs from across the Big Bet Memo Experiments in a stack-ranked hypothesis log. 2. Design and scope a set of experiments to help test these beliefs to form an experiments backlog. 3. Sequence the experiments into a clear roadmap.

In our prior example, a company prioritized building a billing system over validating market demand and unit economics. Had they conducted this Big Bet Experiment Planning exercise, they would have found that the experiment for the billing system eliminates the vast majority of ambiguity about how to collect payment from customers. However, they would have also realized that this addresses a low-priority hypothesis, while consuming a significant amount of the available testing resources. This realization likely would have resulted in a different testing plan.

THE EXPERIMENTATION FIELD IS SET

Leveraging the Big Bet Experiment Planner, the high-value, risk-forward testing now has the right environment in which to accomplish its mission—eliminate or confirm the largest risks relative to value and effort to test.

Are there other important environmental factors to consider for Big Bet success? What are the fundamentals separating good teams from great teams?

CHAPTER 5

CHAMPIONSHIP HABITS

"Champions don't do extraordinary things, they do the ordinary things better than anybody else."

—CHUCK NOLL

John Rossman spent countless hours watching water polo matches as his two sons competed from youth through college. During practice sessions, one coach would frequently emphasize the importance of teamwork, fundamental technique, diligent effort, and staunch defense by exclaiming, "That's a championship habit!" These are the often-overlooked fundamentals and uncelebrated elements that are not directly recorded as a player statistic, yet are crucial for performing and triumphing at the highest level. These are the fundamental habits that win championships.

Thus far *Big Bet Leadership* has served as a guide for succeeding where most executives and companies fail in major transformations by defining counter-traditional philosophies and supporting techniques. Not this chapter. Instead, we revisit some basics; the foundations of most leadership playbooks. While we have focused on the edgy use cases and clear thinking, the critical elements of communication and team culture may seem to have taken a backseat. This chapter is dedicated to re-emphasizing those two cornerstones of Big Bets. Our chapter begins, however, with a tale of defeat.

A GATES FOUNDATION BIG BET

John was deeply involved in one Big Bet that failed to live up to its promise. As a partner at a management consulting firm, John led a consulting team at the Gates Foundation for several years. The biggest of the Big Bets he contributed to was called InBloom. Regrettably, for all of us, it failed.

InBloom was an EdTech start-up funded with a $100 million set of grants by the Gates Foundation in 2011, and shut down in 2014. The promise was to scale personalized instruction by using data and apps via a centralized cloud architecture, deployable to school districts and teachers.

Why did InBloom fail? Could it be that a centralized cloud architecture was not giving state or local districts data governance or the control they desired? Might be. Could it be that the unique funding opportunity and environment that the federal Race to the Top grants contributed led to skipping core assumption and approach trial testing? Possibly. A more iterative and minimum viable product (MVP) approach might have helped. Was InBloom providing potentially threatening data highlighting teacher and district effectiveness? Could be.

Any of these could be rationally argued.

Upon reflection, the significant misstep for InBloom was likely failing to control the story.

Perhaps with a bigger investment in proactive communication and engagement the naysayers might have been converted, or a balanced, better-informed conversation might have ensued. The case study titled "The Legacy of InBloom," conducted by think tank

Data and Society, found that opposition to the project emerged early, fueled by the charges that student data would be exposed, possibly sold to third parties, and even leveraged to block some students' future progress.

It was message of data mistrust. And it stuck. The opposition outflanked InBloom. One Gates senior program officer summarized the postmortem in this way: "InBloom did not have a privacy problem. InBloom did not have a parent problem. InBloom had an advocacy and perception problem."[1]

Over $100 million in grants from the Gates Foundation were lost. Credibility lost. More important, perhaps a once-in-a-generation opportunity to transform US K–12 education, lost.

How can your Big Bet avoid that fate?

By elevating—not sidelining or downplaying—the work of communication and storytelling.

AGAIN, AND AGAIN, AND AGAIN

A Big Bet needs a particular communicator at the forefront: the chief repeating officer.

Of Jeff Bezos's several brilliant capabilities, one that does not get mentioned often is his strategic communication. For example, Amazon's 1997 shareholder letter is the baseline for what Amazon believes in and what it will optimize for. In this first shareholder letter, Bezos communicated Amazon's core beliefs and encouraged potential investors to not invest in Amazon if they were not aligned with these principles.

The letter began with this: "But this is Day 1 for the Internet and, if we execute well, for Amazon.com," and continued, "Because of our emphasis on the long term, we may make decisions and weigh tradeoffs differently than some companies. Accordingly, we want to share with you our fundamental management and decision-making approach so that you, our shareholders, may confirm that it is consistent with your investment philosophy."

What followed was essentially Amazon's long-term investment philosophy and orientation to optimize for long-term results, not short-term optics. And then he repeated it. The 1997 shareholder letter was attached to every subsequent shareholder letter, reminding employees and investors of the mission.

Bezos took the repetition a step further. Bezos turned the Day 1 phrase into a rallying cry. Although "It's still Day 1" is not the mission statement of Amazon, Bezos repeatedly still uses this to rally his team. This simple repeatable "Day 1" chant is so important that an Amazon office building is named Day 1.

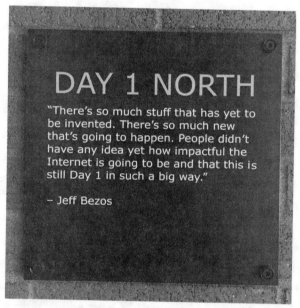

DAY 1 NORTH

"There's so much stuff that has yet to be invented. There's so much new that's going to happen. People didn't have any idea yet how impactful the Internet is going to be and that this is still Day 1 in such a big way."

— Jeff Bezos

Plaque on Amazon Day 1 North Building. *Photo courtesy of author.*

This is what chief repeating officers do. They beat the communications drum with an appropriately short, crafted, outcome-oriented message to build and keep alignment and focus. The messages are not platitudes or jargon—they are not "empty calories." No, these messages have meaning, definition, and consistency, and are part of a bigger story.

Storytelling is a powerful tool in facilitating business transformation because it humanizes the abstract concepts often associated with change. It not only provides context and clarity but stirs emotions and imagination, helping teams better connect with the vision of the Big Bet. When a story narrates the reasons for change, the journey, and the envisioned future, it becomes easier for teams to remember and comprehend the goals and implications. Stories are more engaging and relatable than dry facts and figures, fostering empathy and encouraging ownership. Through storytelling, team members can visualize their roles within the narrative. It essentially turns the Big Bet from a mandatory corporate priority into an engaging journey.

Everyone on the team has to be able to easily quote the "killer feature" statement. Do it often. Correct people when they don't say it, or say it wrong. Words matter. Start every meeting with a reminder of the killer feature and why a customer will love this solution. Sounds corny, and it might be. It also works.

As you step into the shoes of a chief repeating officer, you are likely to feel as if you are a broken record and that the repetition is beginning to dilute the message. When this happens, double down! The reality is that one is far more likely to under-repeat than over-repeat.

Harvard professor John Kotter found that change agents typically under-communicated their visions by a factor of ten.[2] Wharton professor Adam Grant notes that, on average, employees "might be exposed to 2.3 million words and numbers" in a typical three-month period and that "during that period, the vision for change was expressed in only 13,400 words and numbers: a 30-minute speech, an hour-long meeting, and a memo." Grant adds, "Since more than 99 percent of the communication that employees encounter during those three months does not concern the vision, how can they be expected to understand it, let alone internalize it?"[3]

The chief repeating officer must take advantage of the way in which humans process information: the more often we encounter an idea, the more we like it.

The next critical question to ask is this: What should I be repeating? There is a skill to this. Good leaders often make the mistake of delivering empty calories in their communications. "We are going to become an agile organization" or "The patient experience will be reinvented" are classic examples of empty calorie repeated messages. They are useless because they say we are going someplace, but the location is horribly vague. Here, too, research into cognitive psychology points the way, and has influenced how the Big Bet playbook was designed.

We have been party to scores of corporate initiatives seeking to deliver trajectory-changing impact on a business. When crafting communications plans for these initiatives, we have witnessed 90 percent of the initiative sponsors building their internal communication plans around a "burning platform" concept—essentially a complaint about the dangers of the current state of affairs.

Using a burning platform communication strategy focuses on the problem without creating clarity about the solution. As authors Chip and Dan Heath point out in their book *Switch: How to Change When Change Is Hard*,[4] the importance of burning platforms in driving change is a myth! Not only are burning platforms not needed to inspire lasting change; they can be counter-productive.

So, if a burning-platform-driven message isn't the right approach, it isn't the message worth repeating. What is?

Instead of focusing on a burning platform, look to the Big Bet memos. These provide a focus for organization and prioritization. Leverage the clear and compelling future state and the risk-forward experimentation approach—the Big Bet Vector—to build a *Big Bet Communications Quiver.*

A QUIVER?

People who experience the transition from novice to aficionado for a sport are likely to be familiar with the concept of building a quiver. Surfers, snowboarders, skiers, cyclists, and even runners all have a quiver, which is simply a selection of equipment enabling them to match the right equipment to the right conditions. Runners will have race shoes, which are super-light, but wear out quickly; training shoes, which are heavier but more durable; and trail shoes with rugged slip-proof tread. Surfers may have a long board for smaller-wave days and a short board for the bigger swells. Skiers and snowboarders have different equipment for powder days versus packed snow. The intent of a quiver is to ensure that you have the right equipment for the dynamic conditions.

A Big Bet leader needs the same collection of targeted communications in their Big Bet Communications Quiver. Just as a surfer wants to have the board that's needed rather than run to a rental shop when a big swell is coming in, Big Bet leaders want to have each element of the communications quiver on hand to deploy at a moment's notice.

For empirically backed inspiration on how to effectively craft a communications quiver, we look again to *Switch*. The Heath brothers' research pinpoints the most effective hacks for driving change. The following subset of those hacks is particularly relevant for managing Big Bets:

- Find the feeling.
- Point to the destination.
- Script the critical moves.
- Shrink the change.
- Find the bright spots.
- Rally the herd.[5]

Let's discuss the elements to add to the Big Bets Communications Quiver, how they can deliver against those change-management hacks, the conditions to deploy them against, and how to craft them quickly by utilizing the Big Bet Memo Experiments that the team already has on hand.

MISSION STATEMENT

It is important to "find the feeling" when trying to motivate an organization to commit to hard changes over a sustained period—which is exactly what it will require to successfully take a Big Bet from concept to scale. "Finding the feeling" is about tapping into the emotional side of decision-making as a complement to appealing to individuals' reason.

Mission statements are an effective tool for defining the identity in a manner that can be deployed consistently by a chief repeating officer—and by everyone else on the team.

Each of Elon Musk's companies has a clear mission statement outlining a massively transformative purpose (MTP). These mission statements are highly effective at "finding the feeling" and appeal to employees' and shareholders' sense of identity:

SpaceX: To revolutionize space technology, with the ultimate goal of enabling people to live on other planets.

The Boring Company: The Boring Company creates safe, fast-to-dig, and low-cost transportation, utility, and freight tunnels. The mission: solve traffic, enable rapid point-to-point transportation, and transform cities.

Tesla: Accelerating the world's transition to sustainable energy.

These companies' mission statements tap into strong feelings—excitement about exploring the final frontier, avoiding the frustration with soul-destroying traffic, a passion for saving the environment. Employees, customers, and investors can clearly tie these corporate mission statements to their own personal sense of identity and thus, research suggests, they will be more likely to work to overcome obstacles to bring the missions to life. This is the kind of commitment that you want to bring for your Big Bet. The first addition to your communications quiver is a mission statement.

Anyone who has been part of crafting a mission statement probably knows that it can be a tedious and even distracting process. Fortunately, Big Bet leaders already have a strong start. Build the mission statement for a Big Bet using the killer feature and compelling arguments why customers will love the new capability. The mission statements for each of Musk's companies provide a sense for the killer features at the heart of the respective companies.

A mission statement serves as the driving force behind any initiative, acting as a key support for the Big Bet Vector, charting the course of direction, and enabling the team and stakeholders to maintain a consistent focus. It offers a glimpse of the project's overall objective, path, and desired end result. This is where the importance of aligning with the killer feature comes into play. Every initiative, transformation, strategy, or project should have a mission statement that is aligned with the killer feature. The killer feature—the defining, differentiating, and distinguishing aspect of your project—is what sets the effort apart, ignites interest, and propels success.

An inability to write a compelling mission statement, or writing one that is not compelling, raises a flashing warning sign. Pay attention to it! It's a sign that perhaps the Big Bet Vector isn't well defined yet or is not valuable. If friendly stakeholders don't buy into it, how will it land with actual customers or reluctant participants?

Planned, consistent communications pointing the way to the killer feature–oriented future state of the Big Bet is a critical supporting pillar of leadership for Big Bets.

VALUE PROPOSITION, CRITICAL MOVES, AND THE FUTURE PRESS RELEASE

Appealing to emotions through a mission statement is a great start for your Big Bet Communications Quiver, but is not sufficient in itself. You also need to appeal to reason.

Instead of asking a mission statement to do double duty—appealing to emotions and reason simultaneously—add new tools to the communications quiver. In Microsoft CEO Satya Nadella's words, your goal as a leader is to create clarity. "You can't call yourself a leader by coming into a situation that is by nature uncertain, ambiguous—and create confusion. You have to create clarity, where none exists," says Nadella.[6]

Appeal to reason by pointing to the destination through "destination postcards." Destination postcards are a vivid picture showing what could be possible. They create clarity by defining an outcome in a way the audience can grok—meaning to deeply understand. They don't try to create clarity by defining each step to achieve the outcome; rather, they provide enough clarity around the definition of the future that every member of the extended Big Bet team is empowered to define the path forward for themselves.

The good news is that the destination postcard already exists! It's captured in the Big Bet Memo Experiments as the value proposition. For the illustrative Big Bet covered in Chapter 2, "Play Chess, Not Checkers," the destination postcard is this:

Customers can now buy online and pick up within 10 minutes from ordering. A "recommended items" selection of add-on items accompanies our friendly clerk to the car. The mom with two kids in the car can simply verbally select the additional add-on items. After the bags are loaded into the car, the order total is updated and charged to the card.

There are gold nuggets packed into this value proposition:

- Guaranteed ten-minute pickup service level agreement (SLA).

- Customer does not need to get out of their car.

- Personalized and recommended items, which can be approved by the customer at point of pickup, are brought out with the order.

This is a better superpower value proposition than is typical. For example, it is normal to have a value proposition like "We will create a best-in-class buy online pick up at store capability." What's missing? It's missing distinction as to what the best-in-class capability is. It's missing the Big Bet killer feature.

The prose in the superpower value proposition is already highly visible in nature, making it an effective destination postcard, but it is fine to add imagery in the form of pictures or video to reinforce the effect. In either case, pull the value proposition off the shelf and drop it into the Big Bet Communications Quiver. Repeat it often to create clarity.

The next step is to "script" the critical moves. This motivates by creating a clear, unambiguous roadmap for success. The critical moves are the steps that, if achieved in the near term, will establish a trajectory of success.

Again, the good news for Big Bet leaders is that they can add scripted critical moves to their communications quiver by pulling them from the prior efforts—they are already captured in the Big Bet Experiment Planner. Just as adding visual imagery to your value proposition can create a stronger destination postcard, it is a good idea to repackage the contents of the Big Bet Experiment Planner to tailor the critical moves to the appropriate audience, highlighting the five or so that will best resonate. Reference the Experiment Planner and pull out the top five experiment results that, if achieved, will go the longest way toward bringing the Big Bet to life.

Combining the boldness of the Big Bet and the reason the superpower outcome will be loved by customers while addressing the risk of the bet by testing and refining creates a compelling destination postcard.

As a final step to create clarity, build out a future press release and frequently asked questions, or PRFAQ as Amazon calls it. This technique, sometimes referred to as backcasting,[7] ensures that teams focus on customer needs, clarify the product vision, and address potential challenges before starting the actual development work. This document typically includes two elements:

- A hypothetical press release written as if the product or service has already been launched. It outlines the benefits, features, and value proposition for the customers, helping the team understand the end goal and the target audience.

- A section listing common questions that customers, stakeholders, or the press might ask about the product or service. The FAQs address issues related to pricing, target markets, competition, implementation, and any challenges that may arise. This part of the document helps the team anticipate questions and potential problems, fostering proactive problem-solving.

The future press release and frequently asked questions are an expanded version of a destination postcard. They are used for stakeholders needing deeper understanding of the Big Bet.

SPOTLIGHTS

The mission statement, value proposition, future press release and frequently asked questions provide chief repeating officers with plenty of prepared communication materials to create compelling and authentic information to bring the team during the journey. These materials change occasionally, but not frequently, making them ideal for repetition.

Stopping there in building a communications quiver is fine. However, there are three additional catalysts worth adding to the Quiver through the use of spotlights:

Shrink the Change. Especially in the early days, Big Bet success may feel far away to many in the organization, which can undermine support. To overcome this, "shrink the change" by providing the audience with evidence that success is in fact closer than they originally believed.

Rally the herd. Humans become more open to supporting hard challenges when they see their peers doing it already. No one wants to be the first to jump into the pool, but they also don't want to be viewed as laggards by being the last. Showcasing examples of individuals across the organization "getting with the program" increases the odds of others following suit.

Find the bright spots. By pointing to examples of places where desired changes have already been implemented in pockets of the organization, you build confidence that the changes can be achieved more broadly—and perhaps also create a bit of envy and healthy internal competition.

Implement those catalysts by establishing a semi-regular cadence of communications featuring notable developments for your Big Bet. Consciously use these spotlights to shrink the change, rally the herd, and find the bright spots. Not every communication needs to cover all three bases, but try to deploy each of these at least once per quarter.

For the buy online, pick up in store example a leader could shrink the change and highlight the bright spots through a single spotlight sharing the story of a team that rapidly built a prototype for the ability to update cart totals for items added to the order. An additional spotlight could rally the organization by profiling a store operations leader who proactively designed a scalable solution for storing inventory for add-on items.

Be flexible in the format and timing of these spotlights. Remember that they are a means to an end and not an end in themselves. Don't let creating these spotlights slow the team down. Instead, proactively scan for those catalysts and then package them up as a spotlight and distribute them broadly.

Adding the spotlights to the Big Bet Communications Quiver creates a powerful set of communication tools to bring the organization along. Leaders can deploy this robust and flexible set of communication tools to reinforce the success of a Big Bet, all created with only marginal incremental effort by reusing materials already created by the Big Bet team.

What leaders do with these communication tools—how to lead with them—is the superpower that leaders need to understand. That is the creation of the Big Bet team culture.

THE BIG BET TEAM CULTURE

The mission of a Big Bet is likely distinct from the modus operandi of your business. It's the difference between the US Army and the Green Berets. Both serve a greater mission of defending the United States and the Constitution. But the Green Berets, while being part of the US Army, are the tip-of-the-spear special forces and have their own distinct culture.

Team culture forms the default expectations around how we work and what is expected. The most common culture mistakes are often a failure to be explicit about what these expectations are or attempting to make a culture the right culture for everyone. Culture is especially critical for difficult missions requiring focus, skills, bringing the improbable to life, and making it a good business. You will need to be clear about the culture needed for your Big Bet team.

A CULTURE OF BUILDERS

Back to the Amazon shareholder letter again, but this time, not penned by Bezos. The 2021 Amazon shareholder letter was a passing of the baton as Amazon's new CEO, Andy Jassy, took the helm. One of his key themes was the importance of a culture of builders. Paraphrasing what he wrote: When Amazon says we are a culture of builders, they emphasize the ability to define, design, or construct a capability to create new value for a company. Everyone, at every level, is encouraged and challenged to be a builder.[8]

How can you do that in your own Big Bet? Jassy has laid out the steps:

- Hire right. Look for people who like to invent, create, and experiment.

- Organize work teams to be independent so they can focus and create for that customer they know well.

- Provide tools and permission. Speed, said Jassy, is a leadership choice. Give your teams what they need to make decisions and move forward.

A builder culture demands balance. As Jassy emphasizes, you must have faith in the idea that has not yet been proven, but at the same time, commit to ensuring that your plan is viable.

Meet the MLP. That's the minimum lovable product, a twist on the minimum viable product made famous by Eric Ries's Lean Startup process. An MLP is the one you think the customers will love from the get-go. That's your first launch with the killer feature. Then be ready to iterate quickly.

For many of us, the demand to be a builder is best encapsulated in this simple statement: define the future state. Complaining is not a strategy, and complaining about the current state of affairs or why we can't do something better does not create value. This is what's often called "admiring the problem." Although it's interesting to pontificate about why, for example, a healthcare scenario or experience is suboptimal, a vivid description of a future state experience—the outcome—is much more valuable. We can build against this.

The best innovators are hands-on problem solvers. Elon Musk, in the heat of the battle, spends up to 80 percent of his time solving engineering problems.[9]

Owing to the partner and stakeholder management we enlisted early, an important aspect of the Big Bets team culture is that everyone is a builder. No one just manages the work going on. The Big Bet mission will be demanding, creative, decisive, entrusted with resources, and important to the future of the enterprise.

A CULTURE OF ACCOUNTABILITY

Here's a story about Steve Jobs that is often retold when making a point about accountability.

Suppose you come to work one day and the garbage in your office trash can has not been emptied. You find the janitor and demand an explanation. The janitor says, "The lock on the door was changed, so I couldn't get in to empty your trash can."

That's irritating, but it's a reasonable explanation. The janitor can't do the job if they have not been given the right key. A janitor is allowed to have an excuse, Jobs would say.

But the higher you move in an organization, the more you'll be asked to execute without excuses.

For Steve Jobs, that point on the map was vice president. When you rise to the rank of vice president, you are accountable. There is no longer an excuse. There is no key that should have been provided to you. You are responsible.

This is the culture of accountability. It asks you to look within. What is your reputation? Your professional brand? Are you the leader that delivers hard results in situations of uncertainty, high risk, and dependencies? As the Jedi Master Yoda said, "Do. Or do not. There is no try."[10]

A CULTURE OF BUREAUCRACY BUSTING

Leading the direct Big Bet team is hard enough. Most Big Bets work across the enterprise and partners. If you are leading this type of initiative, you have dependencies. How you manage these is likely a significant predictor of the success of the initiative. Although we worked hard to minimize our dependencies through creating software and lab environments, we likely still have dependencies. We are dependent upon others, inside and outside our organization, to deliver for our purposes. And they likely don't directly report to us. Often, navigating these dependencies exposes us to intractable corporate bureaucracy.

Here is the level of expectations, and the mindset we have learned for delivering hard projects, initiatives, and innovation projects when you have a lot of dependencies:

- Work hard at defining the mission in clear terms and from multiple facets. Check!

- Negotiate and manage unambiguous and clear commitments from others. That means having rock-solid commitments and shared understanding, a great plan—even though you know the plan will change. Trust that everyone will speak directly and be solution oriented. Get everyone to be "all in." You can assume nothing.

- Create hedges if appropriate. For every dependency, evaluate whether there should be a fallback plan—a redundant option. Taking absolute responsibility for every possible dependency is no small task. This is one reason that few leaders have the rigor, determination, creativity, and tenacity to successfully deliver. Many of the recommended steps from prior chapters, such as creating a separate digital software stack to reduce the dependencies on corporate systems and technology staff, help to create better hedges.

- Conduct weekly cross-team status meetings featuring the bad news, meetings that run toward the hard things, not toward the easy topics. We will outline the concept of featuring the bad news in Chapter 8, "Trust Me."

- Trust, but verify. Always ask for the right type of evidence, the type that tests and validates the demonstration that something is "done." If you communicate to the team at the start of the project that "trust, but verify" is one way we manage risks, and that we should all adopt a "trust, but verify" approach, everyone will be operating at a higher level.

Develop appropriate project management and control approaches—and don't get lazy! Having great project hygiene is how you systematize this rigor. Project hygiene includes project status reporting, issue and risk tracking, steering committee communications, budget controls, and scope management—all of the "project management" disciplines that teams and leaders know are important, but tend to get lazy about.

These three elements of culture—be a builder, "no excuses" accountability, and owning your dependencies—results in a team built for tackling Big Bets and the unknown nature of what lies ahead. The team members are resourceful, they are trustworthy, they are optimists, and they communicate needs and expectations clearly and consistently. One last benefit: this culture, especially if the broader executive team joins in, will seep into the broader corporate culture. This is fractals theory at work—big patterns get set from small patterns.

The Big Bet Environment sets the Big Bet up for success. The next section includes three chapters addressing critical failure points during the Big Bet journey by making critical decisions, gaining alignment across the larger organization, and establishing oversight of the Big Bet. This is Big Bet Management.

PART III

BIG BET MANAGEMENT

"Leadership is the art of accomplishing more than the science of management says is possible"

—COLIN POWELL

Welcome to the third and final section of *Big Bet Leadership*, where we dive into three aspects of management designed for the unique challenges that transformations, business model innovation, and other types of Big Bets tend to exhibit. After exploring how to Think in Outcomes and setting the Big Bet Environment, it is time to equip yourself with techniques necessary to maintain velocity on a clear destination. The section focuses on innovative management approaches to complement approaches you are already likely using.

Chapter 6, "Continue, Kill, Pivot, or Confusion," focuses on the importance of the key decision-making moments in a Big Bet. It's crucial for you as a leader to recognize when to change course, double down, or cut your losses. This chapter provides a framework for making tough choices and helps develop the skills needed to evaluate and adjust strategies. By applying this framework, you'll be better prepared to maximize the impact of your Big Bet initiatives and minimize the potential for failure.

Chapter 7, "Canary in the Coal Mine," tackles the often overlooked but essential aspect of gaining deep stakeholder understanding and commitment. A Big Bet can't succeed without getting the best from your organization's key players, and it's your job as a leader to ensure that they're on board from the start. We'll discuss the art of sending your canaries into the coal mine to test for hidden dangers to win over skeptics, foster collaboration, and create cross-organization momentum as you work toward your ambitious goals.

Chapter 8, "Trust Me," focuses on Big Bet performance management. A streamlined and efficient approach is critical for maximizing the return on your investment. It's about more than just managing resources and deadlines—it is about using a skeptic's approach to manage the complex effort, to identify hidden snags while forcing the pace of progress. This chapter provides valuable insights into designing and implementing a structure promoting transparency, accountability, and critical thinking. You'll learn how to strike the right balance between oversight and empowerment, ensuring that your team operates effectively and avoids big surprises

CHAPTER 6

CONTINUE, KILL, PIVOT, OR CONFUSION

"I'll do whatever it takes to win games, whether it's sitting on a bench waving a towel, handing a cup of water to a teammate, or hitting the game-winning shot."

—KOBE BRYANT

The path of a Big Bet leader is riddled with high-stakes "continue, kill, or pivot" decisions. The ability to make the right call at these critical moments can mean the difference between achieving groundbreaking success or wasting time, resources, and clout, while missing out on a winning concept because of a lack of patience or foresight. Careers, including yours, may hang in the balance.

CONFLICTING LESSONS

In 2002, Stewart Butterfield partnered with Caterina Fake and Jason

Classon to pursue a vision for a transformative online gaming experience called Game Neverending. After two years of development, the team realized a photo-sharing feature developed for the game had greater potential than the game itself. The team pivoted and Flickr was born. Yahoo! purchased Flickr for an estimated $25 million just one year later. The team's pivot turned a write-off investment into a modest success.

After serving time at Yahoo!, Butterfield decided to have another go at bringing his vision for a transformative gaming experience to life, launching Glitch in 2011. Rinse and repeat. The team again abandoned the gaming vision, pivoting to monetize an internal team productivity tool. Salesforce acquired Slack for $28 billion in 2021. This time, the team's pivot turned a write-off investment into a gargantuan success.

In both cases, the team deployed similar tactics, recognizing delight among users of a tangential feature, and pivoting their company vision to quickly turn the delightful feature into the focus of a scalable business.

The lesson: Be flexible in your vision but firm in your tactics.

Jeff Bezos knew that establishing third-party selection in new product categories was critical for Amazon, but getting the model right took multiple attempts and patience. On a third attempt in 2002, despite external and internal naysayers, Amazon invested precious resources for the model known as the Amazon Marketplace. Unlike Butterfield's teams, Bezos remained stubbornly committed to the original vision for expanding categories and selection to become the everything store but was willing to try different models. Today, the Marketplace is over 50 percent of all orders at Amazon.

The lesson: Be flexible in your tactics but firm in your vision.

Netflix disrupted store-based DVD rental businesses in the early 2000s. Netflix also almost sank itself with a bungled attempt to spin off its DVD rental business in 2011. Remember the name of this brilliant Big Bet? It was Qwickster.com. At the time, streaming was beginning to take off and Reid Hoffman, co-founder and CEO, decided that the businesses and customers for the two services were fundamentally different. Customers protested and the stock lost 57 percent over two months.[1] Netflix did an about-face. Said Hoffman, "There is a difference between moving quickly—which Netflix has done very well for years—and moving too fast, which is what we did in this case."

The lesson: Slow down on big decisions. Truly Big Bets take patience to get right, and acting rashly can sink them before they have a chance to prove their worth.

Our last story is a cautionary tale of the once venerable General Electric and their digital platform strategy. Their industrial Internet of Things platform was called Predix, which was envisioned and loudly marketed as the industrial internet platform to connect machines, operations, and algorithms together. In 2016 GE set off by placing a series of public commitments against this grand vision. They predicted \$15B in revenue from Predix by 2020.[2] Regrettably, marketing and forecasting cannot compensate for the lack of a compelling product, value proposition, or customers. By 2020, they had spent \$7B on Predix, had revenues of \$1B, and Jeff Immelt, the CEO, was on his way out.

The lesson: Prove the market before making big commitments, especially to investors.

So, wait, what is it? Be firm in tactics, but flexible in vision, like Butterfield and team? Be firm in vision, but flexible in tactics, like Bezos? Be patient, do not act too rashly, like Netflix? Or shut down struggling bets quickly and move on to avoid disaster, like GE's Predix?

The reality is that making effective continue, kill, or pivot decisions is hard . . . really hard. Hindsight is 20/20, and the set of lessons learned from anecdotal look-back exercises like the preceding examples are confusing and conflicting. Yet serial Big Bet leaders like Jeff Bezos, John Legere, Satya Nadella, and Elon Musk lead organizations that routinely navigate these crucial decisions, getting them right at a much higher rate than most. How do they do it?

Here are three lessons to help get continue, kill, or pivot decision points right.

BIG BET LEADERS KNOW THEIR ROLE

The most white-knuckled, high-stakes meetings for a Big Bet are the high-stakes continue, kill, pivot decision meetings. Beware of the traps, ambushes, land mines, trip wires, and rigged elections—most executives eventually encounter them all. In gatherings disguised as meetings for collaborative dialogue, progress review, and proposal selection for the next steps with the Big Bet, the sharks invariably prey on the whales.

The setup is often with the entire executive team, the Big Bet directly responsible individual, and other key players. The meeting purpose—whether explicit or implicit—is to choose one of four outcomes:

Continue—invest in the next phase of building, testing, and validating the Big Bet, incorporating lessons learned in continuous pursuit of the vision outlined in the Thinking in Outcomes work.

Kill—shut down current efforts on this Big Bet.

Pivot—make a significant adjustment in the Big Bet, likely redoing the Thinking in Outcomes work.

Confusion—There should be only three outcomes. Regrettably, the fourth outcome not only exists, but occurs too frequently.

It is during these continue, kill, pivot decision meetings that executive leaders overseeing big bets routinely fall prey to a common and destructive failure mode: micromanagement. Executive leaders treat these decision-making moments as an opportunity to audit the Big Bet team's choices, correct mistakes, and second-guess decisions. This creates a dynamic in which the team bleeds velocity and loses an ownership mindset. The team stops making meaningful decisions, elevating all decisions to senior leaders during continue, kill, pivot progress reviews. Distracted by personally managing the minutiae, executives take their eye off the most crucial decision of all: continue, kill, or pivot?

In contrast, effective Big Bet leaders know their roles, and stay in their swim lanes. Instead of using continue, kill, pivot decision meetings as an opportunity to play down a level or demonstrate how they might have done things differently by temporarily co-opting the roles of the Big Bet DRI and team, they keep their eyes on the prize. Effective leaders use these key meetings as an opportunity to deliver against three executive-level responsibilities:

- Reject lazy thinking.

- Pay attention to the *right* details.

- Find the hidden jewels.

Delivering against these executive responsibilities with consistency dramatically increases the odds of Big Bet success.

EXECUTIVE RESPONSIBILITY #1: REJECT LAZY THINKING

Big Bets present a unique set of management challenges. They are different in many angles including this: they exercise different management thinking and skills. Applying typical thinking to atypical situations leads to bad results. It is lazy thinking. Big Bet leaders are responsible for spotting lazy thinking and stopping it in its tracks. Here are six common lazy thinking patterns to identify and reject when evaluating a major decision on a Big Bet.

Just Say No . . . to Abandoning Strategic Imperatives
Throughout the 2010s, the telecom industry remained relatively undisturbed by the fast-paced digital disruption that was toppling one giant after another in other industries. However, telco executives stayed up at night worrying that they would be next.

Late in the decade, one such telco set out to disrupt itself by creating a separate, digitally native start-up. They formed a team and started working on a Big Bet. Then major organizational changes came about, accompanied by budget pressures. A company-wide portfolio review questioned whether the internal start-up should continue, pivot, or cease to exist. Lacking a clear executive sponsor due to the organizational changes, no one stood up to champion continued investment in this bet, which was designed to further an enterprise-level strategic imperative to guard against digital disruption. The Big Bet was killed, the team shut down, the learnings lost.

Not surprisingly, sleepless nights worrying over the threat of digital disruption didn't go away when the Big Bet team was shut down. What had changed was that the company was no longer "in the game." The learnings had stopped; the thinking was not advancing. Eventually, executives recognized that this was a game the company could not afford to sit out and launched new initiatives aimed at making up for lost time—initiatives that were undoubtedly riskier and more expensive due to the price paid to play catch-up.

There will be Big Bets in promising opportunity spaces that never prove themselves out. Generally, these should be shut down, no regrets. However, most companies are facing a handful of strategic imperatives that they know they must get right. When that's the case, it's critical to stay in the game, just as Bezos did with Marketplace. If a bet isn't working out, pivot. Pivot again. And again. Take "kill" off the table as an option. Keep the bet—or bets—small until the right formula emerges. But don't abandon strategic imperatives by emptying the initiative pipeline. It will be much riskier and costlier when the company inevitably plays catch-up later.

Just Say No . . . to the Innovator's Dilemma

Having patience for incubated businesses is a hidden power of Big Bet leaders. In 1997, Microsoft launched a local search website named Sidewalk. Because they did not know how to manage a small, incubated business next to their at-scale and growing businesses, they decided to exit and sold the business to CitySearch in 1997. "Sidewalk was really aimed at what we now call local search . . . Sidewalk is one we should not have gotten out of"[3] lamented Steve Ballmer in 2007, when it was clear that they had let an early small gem escape. Microsoft has since made several expensive attempts to reestablish a viable search engine business.

This is the classic innovator's dilemma. The dilemma lies in the fact that established companies, which are often focused on meeting the needs of their current customers and maximizing short-term profits, struggle to invest in or adopt disruptive models. This is because these innovations can be risky, require significant resources, and may even cannibalize their existing products or services. As a result, incumbent companies may find themselves unable to adapt to the changing market conditions, leading to their eventual decline or failure.

If customer feedback is promising and your instincts tell you there is a good business to be hatched, be patient. Do not kill too aggressively or scale prematurely.

Just Say No . . . To Lazy Pivots

The same telecommunications company discussed earlier in this section recognized the challenge of sustaining growth in a low-growth industry. In response, the company identified adjacent markets where it believed it had a right to play. Executives prioritized one space above the others, crafted a compelling vision, stood up a team, and embarked on executing against a Big Bet. Smart.

As the Big Bet team shared early results, executives were pleasantly surprised at how the team's initial product generated subscriber acquisition, churn reduction, and cost-efficiency benefits for the core business. But . . . the actual hypothesis of the killer feature and advantaged financial model were not proving out.

Management readily supported continuing, as there were benefits to the core established business. Slowly but surely, the Big Bet became an incremental program by way of a "lazy pivot." The promise of trajectory-changing, beyond-the-core business impact was quietly replaced with promises of incremental, low-risk benefits to the core.

Lazy pivots generally happen when teams consciously or sub-consciously stop pursuing a Big Bet vision in favor of an easier and safer—but smaller—idea, and they do so without permission or acknowledgment of the shift. Effective executives recognize these lazy pivots and put a stop to them. Kill the Big Bet. Take the valu-able concepts and put them into the normal project approval pipeline within the company. Do not allow the Big Bet pipeline to be diluted with incremental concepts.

There is a variation of lazy pivots called science fairs. Science fairs are oriented to the cool bells and whistles being developed, versus proving out the high-value, high-risk elements of a Big Bet.

Just Say No . . . to Zombies

Zombies are Big Bet initiatives that are killed, only to come back to life in a slightly mutated form again and again and again. Zombie ini-tiatives drain resources and energy out of the organization by routinely relitigating decisions and diluting efforts against other priorities.

Some may argue that a "no zombies" policy could unnecessarily inhibit innovation, citing examples of initiatives that were hugely successful after originally being rejected. The lore at Google—part truth, part fiction—is that early in his career, current Google CEO Sundar Pichai pitched the idea that Google should develop its web browser, only to be repeatedly told "no" by senior leadership. Pichai ignored leadership and persisted anyway. The zombie idea became Chrome, and Pichai became Google's CEO.

What is more often the case is that hidden initiatives dilute the ability to focus and accomplish all the committed work and goals in an organization, including the Big Bets. The answer is discipline. If a Big Bet is stopped, you must decide to either reframe it by going back through the Thinking in Outcomes objectives, or not. This creates transparency and accountability and avoids zombies.

Just Say No . . . to Drugstore Cowboys

Drugstore cowboys are initiatives that are all hat, no cattle. There is not a compelling value proposition and capability; there is only an abstract notion of what the product or service does, and the marketing, commitments, and budgets on the initiative are ahead of reality. There is often a lack of a Big Bet leader, the directly responsible individual, to corral efforts with multiple groups feeling the pressure to deliver something, anything, but no one knowing what the "thing" is. The GE Predix digital platform is a notable example of a drugstore cowboy.

The healthcare industry seems to attract many drugstore cowboy transformations. Trumpeting "better care, happier doctors and nurses, and lower costs," they cannot demonstrate their theory of how these three outcomes are defined or how they will be accomplished. They are typically a business-as-usual service but with better marketing materials.

Avoiding drugstore cowboys is straightforward: Do they have answers to the questions posed by Thinking in Outcomes? What is the specific customer pain to be alleviated? What is the killer feature, and what are the high-value, critical-risk operational capabilities? How do we design an advantaged cost model? These questions force critical thinking, design, and choices, and surface marketing-led hype.

Just Say No . . . to Premature Scaling

Product-market fit is an important concept in innovation. Product-market fit occurs when a new product or service has identified a customer base that values its offering, and it can satisfy the needs of that segment well enough to generate consistent demand and growth. The mistake is that while product-market fit is important, it is not sufficient to scale. Other factors such as unit costs, supply chain, and field readiness, among several other factors, also need to be proven to commit to scale.

In 2017 Amazon launched the Amazon Go Store. It is a reimagined customer experience employing Just Walk Out technology. Early forecasts projected that Amazon would scale to three thousand stores in a couple of years. Several years later, Amazon still has just over one hundred stores. While product-market fit has been met, Amazon is still figuring out the profitability of the store format and operations.

Effective Big Bet leaders constantly probe, looking around corners to anticipate whether a Big Bet is on a trajectory to achieve scale. They do this through a clear understanding of unit economics. Yes, that's right . . . unit economics.

Whether your unit is orders, cars, or bytes delivered, unit economics is the source of igniting an excellent value proposition, a great business, and a competitive moat.

Unit economics describes in financial terms the per-unit basis of projected financial performance. It measures the revenue and costs associated with producing, selling, and delivering a single unit of a product or service.

In the experimentation of our Big Bet, we are projecting, looking for evidence and proof points giving high confidence of two aspects of our unit economics:

First, every unit of production more than covers its variable costs with a strong return profile, often a return on a defined cash hurdle rate. If this is true, then the company benefits from every additional unit delivered to customers, or to end users, for internal projects.

Second, the fully loaded unit costs, composed of variable costs and fixed costs, should have a steady decline as the Big Bet scales. The Big Bet team should have line-of-sight to this steady decline of fully loaded unit costs and know how they are going to continue to drive fully loaded unit costs down as scale occurs.

While most Big Bet teams inherently recognize the importance of scalable economics, discipline in pursuing them is less common. Teams often lose sight of the full unit economics of their Big Bet and pursue one subcomponent at the expense of others. This commonly occurs when teams begin throwing marketing and customer acquisition spend at a growth problem. Unit sales and, consequently, revenues benefit and tend to headline at the decision meetings, while the suffering margin results get swept under the rug.

The Big Bet team should be all over the unit economics of the Big Bet. The unit economics should be explained in the Big Bet Financial Memo, and proving scalable economics should feature prominently in the Big Bet Experiment Planner. The lazy thinking risk in the continue, kill, or pivot decision moment is letting enthusiasm for the great technology and reinvented customer experience create a "go big" fever. Again, do not forget the Big Bet Financial Memo. A fantastic Big Bet includes an advantaged cost model and proven business model.

By identifying and avoiding these *Just Say No* traps in the continue, kill, or pivot decisions, the executive is doing their job: avoiding lazy thinking.

Let us discuss the second executive responsibility in these high-stakes decision points.

EXECUTIVE RESPONSIBILITY #2: PAY ATTENTION TO THE *RIGHT* DETAILS

The objective of continue, kill, or pivot moments is to reinforce the critical habits of creating clarity, maintaining velocity, and prioritizing risk and value. In doing so, they validate and refine the Big Bet Vector and prevent minor oversights from leading to significant consequences.

To achieve this, effective leaders pay attention the right details, not the wrong details, of how these meetings are conducted.

The Right Details

In these high-stakes Big Bet meetings, here are the five right details requiring design and execution:

Meeting Hygiene: Document clear expectations on what defines a well-run meeting. This includes effective pre-work, facilitation, and follow-up. Materials intended to be pre-read need to be distributed in advance, and participants need to have "done the homework" by reading those materials. The meeting agenda should emphasize what decisions are to be made. Leadership is required; there must be a chair for the meeting. This person is often the executive in charge of the Big Bet, but not the leaders of the Big Bet. Clearly document decisions that were made and action items, and put in place a formal system to ensure information cascading and action item follow-up.

Meeting Cadence: Establish regular, formal check points for reviewing progress and making continue, kill, pivot decisions. It is surprising how often Big Bets are managed in an ad hoc fashion. That is laziness at work. Quarterly is generally appropriate. Increasing the frequency of meetings can be necessary when faster decision-making is needed; reducing the frequency is not advisable. Scheduling these meetings ahead of time allows the team to prepare effectively and efficiently.

Anchor points: Well-managed Big Bet teams create clarity through their Big Bet Memo Experiments and Big Bet Experiment Planner. These are anchor points that help defend against lazy thinking. Developing these outputs is not a point-in-time exercise, but rather a continuous exercise. They should be living, breathing documents that help keep thinking sharp, grounded, and realistically ambitious. Every formal progress check-in should reference these outputs, including any relevant changes. Changes require scrutiny and formal approval.

Decision rights: Again, there are many decision rights frameworks that work well. Examples include Responsible, Accountable, Consulted, Informed (RACI); Recommend, Agree, Perform, Input, and Decide (RAPID); and decision trees. What does not work is avoiding the issue and muddling through the decision-making process. Choose the decision rights framework best suited to the organization and be explicit in its implementation. Push as many decisions as possible to the Big Bet directly responsible individual and team.

Decision criteria: Beware pre-wired traps. It is tempting to create pre-wired decisions. A pre-wired decision is a commitment that means if criteria A happens, or does not happen, then decision B will be made. An example might be "If 25% of the beta customers renew their subscription, then we will scale the program. If it is below 25%, then we are shutting it down." These types of pre-wired decisions attempt to eliminate the ambiguity of continue, kill, pivot decisions through use of objective criteria. Unfortunately, with Big Bets, no set of objective criteria effectively eliminates ambiguity; what is needed instead is sound business judgment that weighs ever-evolving dynamics to make decisions. Pre-wired decisions can lead to many of the traps discussed.

Create a simple written handbook for managing the Big Bet decision meetings and ensure that all stakeholders read, understand, and abide by it. It should cover the elements discussed in this section, but can include others. Explicitly documenting management expectations goes a long way in preventing Big Bet failures rooted in lazy management. Producing the handbook is not necessarily the job of a Big Bet executive leader; ensuring that it exists and is implemented is.

In short, the fundamentals of setting up decision-making and key meetings are the right details for these key moments. These details are often assumed, but they play a pivotal role in the end game of winning or losing in high-stakes moments.

Now on to the third secret Big Bet hidden ability we can all learn from.

EXECUTIVE RESPONSIBILITY #3: FIND THE HIDDEN JEWELS

In 2004, seeing the threat and opportunity from the early Netflix mail-order DVD business, Amazon launched a mail-order business in the UK and then in Germany. What is the legacy of this subscription business? A reusable subscription billing service that was critical in launching one of Amazon's best Big Bets ever—Prime.

The Amazon business leader for the DVD subscription launch, Jorrit Van der Meulen, reflected in an interview, "I thought we were building a DVD rental business, but it became really clear that what we were building was a subscription billing platform. Maybe not first and foremost, but in Jeff's [Bezos] mind, first and foremost. I was initially super confused by the detailed questions he [Bezos] was asking about the database structure, the tables in the database, the 'get' commands, the APIs, and it was only after much reflection later that I realized, his vision for what this subscription billing system was actually going to process in the future was far, far, far more substantial than a DVD rental business."[4]

The DVD rental business subscription engine could have been built in a point solution and narrow manner. Instead, they built a generalized service with the DVD rental business being the first outcome for it to power. Sure, they could have built it a bit cheaper and faster . . . and there was a ton of schedule pressure to launch the DVD business. Instead, when the Prime service concept came up a short time later, the subscription billing service was already built.

Bezos was partially thinking about the DVD subscription business, and partially thinking about future options, scenarios, and reuse. This hidden pattern of zeroing in on the critical value proposition and killer feature and delighting the customer coupled with designing and building in a generalized, flexible manner is a critical leadership technique.

The famous Big Bet leaders we have referenced, including Musk, Nadella, and Bezos, all have an uncanny ability of zeroing in on the hard, first-principle-oriented challenge, design, or architecture component, contributing to the approach and spotting unrecognized hidden opportunities.

As part of the continue, kill, pivot decisions, creating space for design, architecture, and tooling discussions helps to both prepare for scaling and find hidden jewels. The following are some factors to consider.

"Ity" is a suffix meaning "having the quality, state, or degree" of an element. To both consider what is needed for scale and find the hidden opportunities, evaluate which of these elements need focus:

- **Secur-ity:** Keeping out what you want to keep out; keeping in what you want to keep in. Isn't that security?

- **Interoperabil-ity:** Graceful integration and interaction with other types of technology, particularly different brands of technology, and external systems. APIs are one way of creating interoperability for data and processes across an enterprise and enterprises.

- **Measurabil-ity:** The instrumentation and monitoring capability of the system, to allow you to identify, report, and even predict how well things are running and where challenges or failures might be. This can help IT operations as well as business processes dependent on measures, such as tolling or billing.

- **Traceabil-ity:** The ability to track, audit, or explain how transactions, decisions, and systems processes have occurred. "Reconciliation" is not sexy, but critical for control and improvement.

- **Extensibil-ity:** The essential quality of being able to efficiently meet future business needs with as little cost, time, and effort as possible.

- **Qual-ity:** The notion of a system doing what is expected. In technology, key enablers include the ease of being able to test and verify, deploy, manage versions, and effectively deal with software bugs.

- **Stabil-ity:** The ability to deal with new requirements and operating dynamics while not affecting the underlying architecture. Proper abstraction in the architecture design is the key to achieving stability. In the physical environment of computers, networks, and data centers, stability also is reflected in redundancy, failover, and disaster recovery scenarios.

- **Availabil-ity:** The ability to respond immediately. As ESPN football analysts often say about athletes and injuries, "the best ability is availability." Systems and operations must be built for high availability and performance.

- **Separabil-ity:** Creating discrete, well-defined, and separated functions of capabilities in software. A solution typically integrates multiple module services together. An important strategic notion at Amazon is that modular services need to be "self-service"—that is, to use your capability, someone should not need to talk to you to understand, design, test, deploy, or operate your service. This helps not only scale the technology, but also scale the organization.

Understanding how capabilities are designed—the architecture—is an asset for both the Big Bet and for potential future opportunities. The Big Bet team may need help in spotting the implications of an underlying architecture or design approach.

Looking for the valuable, reusable assets and creating flexibility by understanding the fundamentals, which are the first principles of key components of the engineering or operations, is where these hidden assets are found.

HIGH-STAKES MOMENTS

Taking a Big Bet idea from concept to scale involves thousands of decisions. But not all decisions are created equal. Some decisions do matter more than others, and the decision to continue, kill, or pivot is as high-stakes as it gets for a Big Bet. Leaders who get these continue, kill, pivot decisions right—a lot—avoid micromanaging the Big Bet team and instead lean into executive-level responsibilities to reject lazy thinking, pay attention to the *right* details, and find hidden jewels. This rigor results in a decision that, while involving risk, has the best odds of being right.

With an executive-level decision-making foundation in place, the next management challenge to tackle is the often overlooked but essential topic of gaining deep stakeholder understanding and commitment. It is time to surface the dangers lurking within the broader business itself that pose dangers to your Big Bet.

CHAPTER 7
CANARY IN THE COAL MINE

"Guard against the impostures of pretended patriotism."

—GEORGE WASHINGTON

We all know the signals sent by the type of people who say one thing when it's what they're not saying that's more important. There is sincere head nodding, a false façade of agreement, often followed with a message of misdirection such as "I understand," "We will do all we can to support this initiative," or "You can count on my team." These survivors of past corporate transformations are holding their cards tight for now, to be revealed at a future point when it serves their purposes. Welcome to corporate politics and maneuvering, as well as to ways to surface the below-the-waterline snags that can sink a Big Bet.

This chapter is about investing to mitigate the impact of one of the biggest enemies of Big Bet success: tacit internal misalignment and a lack of precise agreement among peers and stakeholders within the organization who control the key resources and decisions required to bring the Big Bet to life at scale. They do not grok the subtle and pointed differentiators and constraints of your Big Bet, nor do they fully buy into your Big Bet approach, but are unwilling to say so.[1]

Let us bring the challenge to life though an example.

A CAUTIONARY TALE: THE HIGHLY EFFECTIVE BIG BET ROADSHOW THAT WAS WHOLLY INEFFECTIVE

Josh was brought into a Fortune 500 company to lead Digital. "Digital what?" you might wonder. Yeah, as is all too common for leaders with "digital" in their title, that wasn't clear. Most of the incumbent senior leaders at the company would quickly agree that it meant that Josh owned managing the enterprise website and core customer mobile applications. These two represent essentially the thin veneer put in front of the customer. But then they quickly made it clear that anything else in their existing responsibilities was not part of Josh's scope—anything below the thin veneer of the customer applications.

Josh had a more expansive point of view. He didn't view digital as just a website or mobile app. Instead, he viewed digital as anything that impacted the customer experience—provisioning, service, billing. He also saw the opportunity in impacting the future of work across the business, and how they competed in the market. His aspiration was to lead, largely by influence, a digital transformation of this substantial public company.

Josh set about defining the business's digital transformation outcome. His team defined a set of delightful, digitally enabled customer experiences projected to drive long-term revenue; identified how digital would transform the company's cost structure; and established strong analogs from within and outside the industry to bolster the case for a full digital transformation. They developed high-quality presentation materials, including visually compelling video clips, to make the case. The logic, quality, and convincing nature of this work was an example of what "good" looks like—some of the best examples we've encountered in the last two decades.

By conducting an internal roadshow, Josh's team made every effort to disseminate information, obtain feedback, and foster excitement about their digital transformation Big Bet. They discussed their vision with not only the highest level of the company's leadership, but also with those three levels down during EVP Town Hall meetings. The organization demonstrated united and enthusiastic backing for the team's vision.

Mission accomplished, right?

Unfortunately, no.

Emboldened by this broad and enthusiastic support, Josh's team set about an aggressive roadmap bringing their vision to life. They got to work in launching Phase 1 of their transformation effort. For the first three months, everything seemed to be going according to plan. At first slowly and then quickly, the foundations of support that they thought had been built and solidified crumbled.

What happened? As is the norm more than the exception for Big Bets, it wasn't any single element or factor that derailed Josh's digital transformation. It was a death by a thousand cuts, small losses, and the tide shifting from enthusiasm to neutral. Those enthusiastic supporters never became outright antagonists. Instead, they purposely or inadvertently undermined the effort by introducing delays and compromises at every step, bleeding the transformation of velocity and impact. They backed their enthusiastic words with passively resistant actions.

One fundamental factor contributing to the declining support for this Big Bet was the failure to establish an appropriate performance management system, which is the story of Chapter 8, "Trust Me." Stakeholders should not have been able to openly support an idea without simultaneously making real priorities and commitments. That said, Josh's team committed a prior mistake during the roadshow as they attempted to build support. When they shared their captivating vision with vital stakeholders within the company, their engagement style did not solicit the type of discerning feedback required to make sure they were truly communicating.

This chapter addresses what Josh's team did wrong and how to avoid making the same mistake.

ASK THE RIGHT QUESTIONS

Josh's team made the mistake of presenting a highly compelling vision to their audience and asking a perfectly obvious question: What do you think? It's the question most anyone would ask. The intent was to get feedback from stakeholders about what might not work or what they might not be willing to actively support. Providing that input was the task implicitly assigned by Josh's team to their audience.

The framing of the question as "What do you think?" resulted in an overly demanding task for the stakeholders. Especially with the high quality of work that went into presenting the vision, a compelling story, and logic prepared with the slide-making genius of a high-end strategic consulting firm, the audience didn't stand a chance in finding flaws. The positive feedback was a *fait accompli*—preordained and essentially, though inadvertently, rigged.

Advocating for a digital transformation was pushing through an open door, and no one was going to stand up and say "I don't think we should attempt a digital transformation." It was like asking a group of doctors if one should start exercising and eating a balanced diet. With the quality of the vision Josh's team had created, no one could resist or find significant fault. That felt like success to Josh.

But there was more going on than Josh realized—and his questions were not surfacing the nonobvious but vital information. Despite their apparent approval, most stakeholders disagreed with key points behind Josh's approach. Worse, the "dis-agreers" were not aligned in their points of disagreement. The CFO wasn't sold on the price tag. The CIO wasn't sold on the roadmap. The chief strategy officer and her reports all disagreed with the plan to hire the consultancy to run the transformation. Yet none of these points of misalignment were voiced to Josh, because the stakeholders involved didn't want to hold up or combat the entire vision based on their particular concerns.

They figured they could work to reshape those individual elements of the plan when the time was right. It was in their best interest to be vocal supporters now and get to their concerns later.

None of the critical senior members of the executive team had time to prepare a counter-proposal to match the rigor and depth of Josh's proposal. To take on debating his proposal would be like showing up with a knife to a gun fight. The effort involved in providing input on the vision was too high. So they just didn't do it, figuring that they would more discreetly steer decisions in the right direction over time. And that's how Josh's digital transformation got set up to die a death by a thousand cuts.

If "What do you think of our vision?" is the wrong question, what is the right question? When getting critical feedback and support across broad stakeholders, how do we not just inform them and get their general agreement, but actually make a committed decision together? The answer is to offer three scenarios.

By creating three valid yet different scenarios of the digital transformation, the critical stakeholder engagement surfaces real concerns and helps the stakeholders understand and debate true options, creating the environment and setting that will result in far better decisions and alignment. Here's how Josh's team could have reframed their approach.

"We all know that this company needs a digital transformation. But there is no single vision or path to success in driving a digital transformation. We have developed three compelling future state visions and paths forward, three scenarios, all of which share some commonalities, but with important and distinct differences around key choice points. We want your input on three questions:

"Which scenario would you recommend?

"Why would you specifically recommend that scenario?

"For each of the other two scenarios, what would have to be different for you to choose the scenario?"

This reframing and contrast greatly reduces the effort involved for your audience to provide useful input while forcing them to assert a perspective beyond the fluffy "I like it!" Your audience does not have to create an alternative scenario to defend against your well-formed vision—you have done that work for them, which is your job as the Big Bet leader. By creating three scenarios, contrast is introduced, providing useful surface area for getting feedback from internal stakeholders.

Three scenarios coupled with better questions increases your chances of converting the thin early alignment into honest overt misalignment. The points of misalignment need to be addressed, but by coaxing sources of misalignment out of hiding you have a much better chance to see them coming and effectively combat them when they arrive, heading off slowdowns or impact-sacrificing compromises. In much the same way that we have brought key capability risks forward to the start, we have now created better understanding, communication, commitment, and strategic decisions.

SCENARIO ANALYSIS: A DOUBLE-EDGED SWORD

There are many traps in scenario analysis. Scenario analysis can be a highly productive catalyst for advancing your Big Bet—or it can be a major source of analysis paralysis, false precision, and as one wise client voiced to John, just an exercise in calculating yourself rich.

Scenario analysis is a risky endeavor because it is highly prone to analysis paralysis, yielding not one but three visions to analyze to death! Scenario analysis can increase instead of decrease the ambiguity as people lose track of which scenario is being pursued.

In our experience, nine times out of ten, scenario analysis does not provide critical value and becomes an academic exercise. Not only does the exercise consume resources and effort while failing to advance the Big Bet; scenario analysis can move the Big Bet in the wrong direction.

The trick to using scenario analysis as a force for good is to—you guessed it—apply smart constraints to the exercise, ensuring that it stays true to the purpose of advancing the critical decisions for the Big Bet. You can achieve this through the *Big Bet Three Futures Memo*.

THE PURPOSE OF THREE FUTURES

Before diving into what a Big Bet Three Futures Memo is and how to craft it, let's start with defining its purpose and highlighting a few common pitfalls to avoid.

As with every Big Bet approach in this book, the intent of the Big Bet Three Futures Memo is to clarify and maintain the vector of your Big Bet. The purpose of this exercise is to sharpen the Big Bet Vector, surface meaningful points of misalignment from within the organization, and maintain velocity by surfacing future organizational roadblocks, bottlenecks, and impact-sapping compromises. Armed early, you are equipped to mitigate the risks before they materialize. Surfacing misalignment creates clarity by putting the collective knowledge, intuition, and experience of your organization to work in identifying the blind spots, weaknesses, and false assumptions that reside in your Big Bet. These always exist.

A frequent challenge in implementing scenario analysis is getting co-opted by ulterior motives or reassigning the exercise to complete a different purpose. There are two common traps that scenario analysis often falls into, each with parasitic purposes or motives:

Trap 1: The Goldilocks Trap. When presenting a vision to the organization, leaders may fall into the bad habit of focusing on convincing their audience that their idea is the right idea instead of using the exercise to solicit useful feedback from the stakeholders to help refine and improve their idea. This "convincing-everyone-we're-right" purpose often loves scenario analysis and utilizes a common sales tool to advance its agenda: the Goldilocks framing of three scenarios. The Goldilocks trap occurs when the audience is presented with a poor-quality option, an unrealistic option, and a "just-right" option. While this is effective at getting the audience to agree that the just-right option is the best of the three, the exercise is rigged and is ineffective at surfacing valuable points of misalignment. This is a fantastic way to get early sign-off on a plan that will not ultimately be backed by supporting actions.

It is a waste of time to ask stakeholders if they prefer scalding hot porridge versus comfortingly warm porridge, or a brick house versus a straw house. As the Big Bet Three Futures Memo is crafted, make it hard for the audience to choose a scenario. Each scenario should be highly compelling, but for different reasons that are clearly articulated. Doing that makes an engaging exercise for the audience, resulting in higher-quality inputs.

Trap 2: The Crystal Ball Trap. A different trap is the Crystal Ball trap, which attempts to utilize scenario analysis to predict the unpredictable future. These exercises revolve around a spreadsheet full of assumptions and calculations. They produce three sets of input assumptions with three sets of corresponding output assumptions. The purpose becomes trying to predict the future by soliciting input into which set of assumptions is right. The problem? They're all wrong because we can't predict the future.

Don't try to create a fine-tuned prediction of the future early in a Big Bet. You'll be wrong, no matter what. Model-driven scenario analyses provide a false sense of comfort through the assumption that a robust, data-and-analytics-driven approach has created clarity, when it actually cannot. These exercises miss factors that cannot be modeled, such as organizational readiness or many aspects of adoption or new revenue forecasting. A few tweaks to an assumption here and another there dramatically changes the outputs. Predictably, this exercise becomes a goal-seeking exercise. It creates an illusion of rigor that is hard to argue against. The major points of misalignment will, again, remain hidden, waiting to eat your Big Bet implementation for lunch one bite at a time.

What is the effective approach for the Big Bet Three Futures Memo?

THE CANARY IN THE COAL MINE APPROACH

Coal miners began carrying canaries into coal mines in 1911. Canaries' heightened sensitivity to deadly but odorless gases such as carbon monoxide, along with their portability, made them ideal early-warning mechanisms—at least until replaced by the "electronic nose" in 1986. [2]

The purpose of your Big Bet Three Futures Memo is to sniff out the noxious, odorless gasses threatening your Big Bet. Of course, you are not actually worried about carbon monoxide. Instead, you are worried about the unstated Big Bet killers that have not surfaced or been articulated; the unknown unknowns. Here are some of the forms that these silent killers can take:

- You are worried that the chief marketing officer will de-fang the killer feature because it is not on brand.

- You are worried that the chief technology officer cheers your success as you get going, only to surprise you with a tentative eighteen-month timeline to fit key systems work into the broader IT roadmap.

- You are worried that the regulatory function blocks your product launch due to potential implications for a tangential regulatory action.

- You are worried that the CFO resists investing to scale because the margin structure does not match that of the core business, even though the ROI is ten times that of the core, accretive to earnings, and creates a new market.

- You are worried that the chief human resources officer (CHRO) does not understand the ten-times implications to productivity that reengineering the knowledge worker jobs across all functions with ChatGPT and generative AI might have.

The job to be done by the Three Futures Memo is to make clear which of those worries are unfounded and which have merit.

WRITING THE BIG BET THREE FUTURES MEMO

Given how often we've seen scenario analysis exercises go wildly astray, let's start with the recommended constraints applied, ensuring that this is a high return on effort (ROE) exercise. Here are the three rules:

Rule #1—Writing the Three Futures Memo takes no longer than five business days of elapsed time.

If starting the exercise on Monday of this week, finish it on Friday of this week. It is critical to keep the project moving at pace and with continuity. Do not bother trying to carve out an afternoon here and a day there. The Big Bet Three Futures Memo is a highly valuable exercise only when it is deliberately kept lightweight. That means giving it a week, not a year's worth of incremental moments.

Rule #2—The team must produce a "Day 1" answer on . . . Day 1 of the exercise.

Early on in a Big Bet, the team is likely small. It consists of a leader plus perhaps a few direct reports helping with research, analytics, and feasibility; perhaps a peer who is co-championing the idea.

Choose one member of the team to be the scribe for the Three Futures Memo. If you are a senior executive with competing demands consuming 90 percent of your time, assign a junior team member who can devote more than 50 percent of their time to the memo. If you can invest the time, we highly recommend that you own the pen yourself. Your intuition in anticipating other senior leaders' thoughts and actions, or inactions, is valuable in crafting the content.

Whoever is acting as the scribe is responsible for producing a "Day 1" draft of the memo the first day, and sharing with the team. When sharing with the team, include the following language:

This is a Day 1 draft of our Three Futures Memo. It needs wordsmithing and better flow. There are numerous placeholders. Some of the content is flat wrong. But it is a start. Please comment in the document aggressively so that we quickly identify the most vital opportunities for making this better.

This type of hypothesis-driven problem-solving is a hallmark of McKinsey's problem-solving methodology and is key to combating analysis paralysis by forcing an early perspective on the final answer.

Rule #3—No more than three pages plus a summary table.

The key is to have zero flex on this constraint. The audience has limited time and attention, so brevity is important. Additionally, this exercise is not intended to be comprehensive in nature; rather, it is a way to frame the thought process to your audience in a way that is conducive to sparking understanding and input, both of which are valuable at an early stage in the life of your Big Bet. By keeping the Three Futures Memo constrained to three pages or less, it is easier to ensure that the reader understands the intended lightweight nature of the exercise, which is focused on big sources of misalignment, not nitty-gritty details that can't be forecasted now.

THE BIG BET THREE FUTURES MEMO

With the preceding rules in mind, let's get on with crafting the Big Bet Three Futures Memo and putting it to work. The goal is to create a pre-read package to share with stakeholders prior to getting input from them on your Big Bet. The good news is that the pre-read materials are nearly complete! Your job is to package up the Big Bet materials that you've already created into a single pre-read package, adding the Three Futures Memo to the end. The complete pre-read package includes the following elements:

- What Sucks? Customer Exploration Framework
- Outcome Definition Memo
- Outcome Financial Memo
- Other People's Outcomes Flywheel Memo
- Big Bet Experiment Planner
- Three Futures Memo

Organize the three-page Three Futures Memo in this manner:

Page 1: Referencing the contents of the pre-read package, highlight the most important elements of the Big Bet's future that you believe hold true under any scenario. Josh and team might have included their highly produced video showcasing delightful future-state customer journeys. Embedding a video is a bit of a cheat, but given that the video was short and clear, we'd be fine with it.

Page 2: Describe a compelling alternative future for your Big Bet, spelling out the specifics of what is different. Be hypothesis-driven to choose differences where you suspect there may be unspoken misalignment.

During the roadshow, Josh's team was very worried about which consulting firm to hire. This was built on a strong belief that the company did not have the internal capabilities required to drive a successful digital transformation. Thus, a key operating imperative that would have been highlighted in their Outcome Definition Memo was for a third-party consulting firm to lead the company's digital transformation. Their second scenario may have described an internally driven effort in which the operating imperative changes from the need to "hire the right consulting firm" to the need to "hire experienced talent." Josh's team might have then highlighted the other elements of the Big Bet pre-read package that could have changed as a result, such as a slower pace of testing that is dominated by a talent-hiring and ramp-up phase for the first six months.

It's okay to include up to five major differences versus the base case scenario, but no more.

Page 3: Page 3 is simply a repeat of the process, introducing a third scenario. Josh's team may have introduced a scenario in which the primary source of value creation switched from backend office efficiencies to customer acquisition and retention benefits.

Summary Table: Create a table summarizing the text from the preceding three pages. Help the reader visualize the elements that are consistent across all three scenarios and those that change. Add an additional column titled "Other?" and an additional row also titled "Other?" You do not need to call attention to these parts of the exercise in the instructions to your audience, but they are good to add to signal that if a reviewer feels strongly about a key element that is missed or an entire scenario that is neglected, they are welcome to provide that input as part of their feedback.

Do not be overly prescriptive regarding the content in each section, as this can lead to teams losing sight of the purpose. Focus on filling the three pages plus the table with the content that most effectively surfaces points of misalignment in your organization.

Here are a few additional guidelines to keep in mind:

- Work hard to make each scenario equally compelling, though not artificially so. This doesn't mean that each has the exact same ROI. Perhaps one has a higher return but more risk. Or a higher ROI but bigger upfront investment. Don't artificially engineer parity across the scenarios.

- Don't create net new content to complete this exercise. Refer to the Big Bet Memo Experiments. Build scenarios off this existing content versus introducing material net new analysis.

- Each option has to be a viable option, and a do-nothing option is not allowed, as it is implicit.

With the memo complete, send it to a small handful of individuals from across roles and functions, focusing on those key enablers of the Big Bet. As you share the Big Bet Three Futures Memo with stakeholders, ask them to read it in advance and share their written answers to the following questions offline:

- Which scenario would you choose?

- What are three explicit reasons this is the scenario you would choose?

- For each of the other two scenarios, what would have to change for you to prioritize it instead?

We suggest placing a time block on calendars for stakeholders to read and provide feedback. Make it no more than one to two hours.

Once you have received the written feedback—not before—schedule a thirty-minute meeting to discuss. This discussion provides an opportunity for stakeholders to ask clarifying questions and may surface new insights.

Share the memo with a diverse set of internal stakeholders, not just the marketing and technology organizations. Include departments such as procurement, legal, and HR that are often forgotten. But don't share the memo with a hundred people—you won't be able to process that much feedback, and much of it will be redundant anyway. Sharing with five to ten people, maybe twenty, is a good rule of thumb.

Most importantly, capture and summarize the feedback you receive. Use the feedback to inform your Big Bet Experiment Planner. Were there missing items? Maybe there were hypotheses on the list that aren't such big sources of risk after all? Maybe you need to adjust the sequencing of experiments. You may be adding new items centered around organizational readiness or capabilities. Any substantive resistance that is surfaced through this exercise is a source of risk to be addressed by a hypothesis on your Big Bet Experiment Planner.

BACK TO OUR FRIEND JOSH

Let's circle back to what might have been different if Josh's team had solicited feedback on three different digital transformation scenarios instead of just one. His team might have chosen to present their roadshow materials exactly the way they did, fancy videos and all, though we do not view that as necessary. Each of their roadshow meetings would have gone the same, including leaving room for active Q&A . . . except for one change. At the end of each presentation, they would have closed with the following ask:

"Thank you for your time and engagement today. As is clear, we all know that our company needs a digital transformation. But there is no single path to success in driving a digital transformation. We have outlined three compelling paths forward, the scenarios, all of which share some commonalities, but with crucial differences around key choice points. We want your input on three questions:

"Which scenario would you recommend?

"What are three explicit reasons why this is the scenario you would choose?

"For each of the other two scenarios, what would have to be different for you to choose that scenario?"

Josh's team would have then emailed the roadshow materials along with the Three Futures Memo to select audience members, requesting that they provide a written response to the three specific questions in a week. The feedback from the chief strategy officer would have centered on the consulting-driven approach, advising to choose Scenario 2 instead. The CTO would have been more likely to raise concerns about the timeline of those delightful customer experiences, challenging the hypothesis that they are early versus late contributors to the overall value proposition. And the CFO may have suggested adding a scenario with a cash-flow profile different from any of the three offered. None of those outcomes are certain to have happened, but by asking for feedback, Josh would have increased the chances of surfacing the sticky points of misalignment that later derailed their Big Bet.

BUT WAIT . . . THERE'S MORE!

Research on the power of scenarios in decision-making highlights an additional, valuable purpose—the "Creative Spark" that the Three Futures Memo can bring.

Scenarios can be used to deal with two worlds: the world of facts and the world of perceptions. They explore for facts but they aim at perceptions inside the heads of decision-makers. Their purpose is to gather and transform information of strategic significance into fresh perceptions. This transformation process is not trivial—and more often than not, it does not happen. When it works, it is a creative experience that generates a heartfelt "Aha!" and leads to strategic insights beyond the mind's previous reach.[3]

The Three Futures Memo generates this secondary benefit while establishing a healthy habit for the team: using the power of scenarios and better questions to expand thinking. However, we caution against promoting the creative spark purpose to the number one priority. Exercises intended to spark creative problem-solving through scenario analysis tend to become heavyweight and lose impact. For example, a scenario-based planning effort that was conducted by the US Coast Guard and was highlighted in a 2020 *Harvard Business Review* article[4] involved a team of consultants working with dozens of senior Coast Guard officials to craft sixteen different scenarios, while engaging hundreds of others in the exercise.

Through this approach of soliciting better feedback on a concept, the coal mine of your Big Bet is safe from poisonous gasses. You can accelerate progress on the Big Bet now that your corporate partners and key stakeholders have participated in Big Bet scenario development, resulting in a refined understanding of the Big Bet and flushing out potential snags of corporate politics. How do you do your job of providing management around the initiative? Let's discuss pressure testing.

CHAPTER 8

TRUST ME

"Trust, but verify."

—RONALD REAGAN

John Rossman's typical morning routine begins with taking his French bulldog, Bossman,[1] outside first thing, then having a cup of coffee and checking emails. Then he's off to the gym. This particular Wednesday was one of these typical mornings. Except, he got an atypical early morning message.

"Hey John, I'm back as CEO. I'd love to catch up and see what direction you might have for me on some challenges I see."

"Sounds serious," John thought.

Ron had been a client ten years prior. At that point the company was just starting to develop a view on how to take advantage of mobile technology and a digital experience for his customers and many hourly gig workers. Clients needed to put people to work, and the gig workers needed to find work and get paid. John had the opportunity to guide the development of this strategy and turn around the technology operations of the organization.

A few years later, Ron had hired a new CEO, done a successful acquisition, driven the digital adoption of a mobile-first experience, been elevated to the chairman role, and was happily semi-retired and sitting on a couple of company boards. But life and business happen in a hurry.

The CEO is dismissed. Ron steps back in as CEO and starts diving deep into day-to-day business and key initiatives. It took him a day to get uncomfortable and call John. The enterprise had a Big Bet to transition from a single vendor providing their mobile technology, front-office applications and key customer experiences to an in-house-built mobile application and a suite of vendor applications, with a vast amount of integration tying end-to-end scenarios together.

After two years of "progress," tens of millions of dollars and nothing delivered to end users, Ron knew the Big Bet was off track, despite the board updates he had been getting. He asked John to assess and make recommendations on what they should do. John framed the engagement as a "pressure test" of the Big Bet initiative. A pressure test is an evaluation of an initiative, squeezing it from every angle, to find where the weak spots are and to get a bearing on the important facets and prospects for a Big Bet.

But how well can you know your Big Bet? Are you hoping it's going well? Do you really know? Can you afford to be wrong? What are your blind spots? What are the unknown unknowns, the risks and issues lurking under the visible waterline like a submarine waiting to torpedo your boat?

How critical is pressure testing on a periodic basis? Consider your biggest Big Bet nightmare.

Imagine the Big Bet initiative doesn't go well. Imagine it is off schedule, off budget, rejected by users, and saddled with team morale issues and infighting. This happens after optimistic progress reports throughout the Big Bet. The critical initiative is not delivering the financial or operational benefits that formed the business case. It's a failure. What's worse, you're the "owner" of this failure.

Imagine you are asked by the company board, "What did *you* do to avoid this disaster?" You could respond with, "I was *told* everything was fine. The status reports were green. I was told it was going well. We held executive updates and frequent status meetings. I did everything I was supposed to do!" And that was true.

Everything on the status reports and board updates indicated progress was on track. Mostly. All green checkmarks. Okay, a few yellow indicators. There was some discussion of challenges and slippages. But the team was confident.

Everything was fine.

Until suddenly . . .

It wasn't.

If you've broken out in cold sweat, you're ready to hear more about pressure testing and truly understanding the weak spots, status, and prospects for your Big Bet.

BIG BETS FAIL—BUT I'M SURE YOURS WILL BE DIFFERENT

The vast majority of transformations fail. According to McKinsey, BCG, KPMG, and Bain & Company, the risk of failure falls somewhere between 70 percent and 95 percent. McKinsey reports that "contributing factors include insufficiently high aspirations, a lack of engagement within the organization, and insufficient investment in building capabilities across the organization to sustain the change."[2]

Your Big Bet is no longer just a concept; it's coming to life. You have conducted memo experiments by Thinking in Outcomes, refining, justifying, and fighting through ambiguity, zeroing in on the specifics by Thinking in Outcomes and supporting critical elements of a future state. A high-judgment leader has been put in charge of the initiative to test, refine, and validate these critical elements.

There are real investments now being made. The number of people directly involved is growing, as is the number of people interested in progress. Resources supporting the Big Bet, including senior leadership and board attention, create consequential opportunity costs to the business—there's a limited number of Big Bets a business can do.

If the Big Bet fails early on while memo experiments are being conducted, there are no real issues to be managed outside the team. Of course, we should understand how our execution of Big Bet Thinking could improve, but we did our job. The Big Bet was not worth pursuing, and we must continue to envision how the wicked problem might be solved or find a more valuable problem to solve for the business.

When the work of building prototypes starts, resources are allocated and the company starts spending real money, perhaps looking beyond the testing of the core concepts into the building and scaling work. Everything takes a step up the logarithmic scale. If the Big Bet fails now for the wrong reasons, it might be a problem. It might be *your* problem. As the senior executive overseeing the Big Bet, you need to make sure that it doesn't fail for the wrong reasons or, if it fails for the right reasons, that you see the failure coming from a mile away. In other words, there should be no surprises.

On a near real-time basis, you want to know if the status of your Big Bet is red, yellow, or green regarding the work being done by the Big Bet team, which is testing the most valuable and critical components of the Big Bet. If red or yellow, you want to be able to clearly identify the issues and whether you are on top of them so that you can lean in where needed.

The team writes progress reports and has scheduled regular status updates, and you think they're making an honest effort to be truthful. However, you also recognize that the team is influenced by decision-making biases, leading them to be naturally overly optimistic and thus vulnerable to blind spots in critical areas or to falling prey to pressures, norms, and biases.

When reading and listening to the team's update, you do your best to ask good questions and to try to look around corners where maybe the team is not. At times, you ask questions of the team that, in retrospect, weren't vital to be addressed now. But because you asked, the team feels the need to get back to you with a solid answer, wasting their time. The same happened with questions from other executives in the room. These status items and ensuing action items now are taking up a meaningful amount of time. You don't want a culture in which the team works to please the executives. You want a mission-driven team looking out for the enterprise and helping you make the best decisions and designs regarding this Big Bet.

What you need is a higher-ROE (return on effort) performance management system for the Big Bet—one that gives you five times the confidence in the Big Bet trajectory and where, specifically, help is needed, while simultaneously requiring 50 percent less time spent on initiative governance and oversight. You need a performance management system setting you up to avoid the avoidable pitfalls, seize value, and make the significant decisions coming from this effort.

Senior leadership and the company boards have two important jobs. The first is to provide oversight and value-added advice to the Big Bet team and the initiative itself to help avoid the blind spots every team and leader has. This is performance and risk management. The second is to prepare the board and executive team to make the continue, kill, pivot decisions.

We write this chapter in general for the overall Big Bet team, but in particular for the CEO, because they are the ones always responsible for the truly Big Bets.

In this chapter, we are not prescriptive on setting up the Big Bet performance management system. But we are defining concepts to address how to fundamentally reshape how to lead, act, and steer Big Bet initiatives—because whatever the big consulting firms are selling on strategic initiative management, it is not working.

These concepts are organized in the five sections of this chapter:

1. Maintain Velocity.
2. Keep Thinking Big.
3. Manage by Proof Points.
4. Create Separation.
5. Feature the Bad News.

Welcome to trust, but verify—Big Bet style.

MAINTAIN VELOCITY

Like the Death Star from *Star Wars* using a tractor beam[3] to pull the rebel ship into its control, there is a consistent invisible pull from the established organization on the Big Bet to normalize, dilute, de-risk, and slow down. The most important job of performance management of a Big Bet is to assist the team in avoiding this slippery and almost irresistible retrenchment to the norm. To avoid this tractor beam, there are three nonnegotiables needed in a Big Bet performance management system to maintain the focus, rapid progress, and mission of the Big Bet.

The first nonnegotiable is to make your availability and efforts for the Big Bet a true priority. Instead of "Let's discuss this at next month's steering committee," the right answer is "Let's meet tonight and make this decision." That is on your top-priority list.

It's shocking how often executives talk about the vital nature of the Big Bet, but a look at their personal time commitment shows it's not really their priority. Jeff Bezos emphasized this point several years ago:

"All of our senior executives operate the same way I do, they operate in the future, they live in the future. None of the people that report to me should be focused on the current quarter. When Wall Street congratulates us for a good quarter, that quarter was baked three years ago. Right now, I'm working on a quarter that's going to reveal itself in 2021. That's what you need to be doing. You need to be two to three years in advance."[4]

Are you guilty of this misalignment? Audit your calendar. If the Big Bet is 5 percent of your total time and attention and you routinely allow Big Bet meetings to be rescheduled, this is a bad sign. Hold yourself accountable for spending 10 to 30 percent of your time each month dedicated to the Big Bet, and make these meetings the top priority.

The second nonnegotiable is to be the heat shield. You must provide a protective boundary around the Big Bet team and priority, deflecting the tentacles encroaching on them. For example, the team is told that corporate officer sign-off to bypass a procurement or HR step is needed. The request is escalated to you and your answer is yes. Today! Or your team needs to attend the mandatory corporate two-day retreat. "Sorry, not this year" is your answer. These requests and business-as-usual situations are just a couple of examples of the little cuts that bleed out momentum and create scope creep.

The heat shield requires a close partnership between the senior executive and the leader of the Big Bet, the DRI. The DRI needs to identify when the team is being asked or influenced in a way that pulls it off-mission or is being burdened with requests and mandates that add risk to execution. Upon recognition of the issue, the DRI seeks to solve it.

As soon as the DRI thinks there might be a situation they cannot quickly solve, they send a clear email to the Big Bet executive explaining the request; why it is risky or counter-mission for the team to absorb the request; the recommendation; and their case for why they should give the team permission to avoid that request, at least for now. Once the email is sent, the DRI should text the senior executive. The Big Bet senior executive reviews the email, agrees or disagrees with the recommendation, and takes on the responsibility of explaining the decision to others.

Escalations like this should be a rarity if stakeholder management is done correctly. If the Big Bet team partners early and often with stakeholders, many of these situations are preempted and escalations are avoided.

The third and final nonnegotiable to maintain velocity is to resist removing or changing constraints. Throughout our journey through the Big Bet, we have outlined key constraints. For example, in creating the Big Bet Memo Experiments, only one killer feature and five operational imperatives were allowed. One elapsed week was allowed for the three futures scenarios to be developed. These constraints are forcing functions to maintain focus on critical and key value drivers and differentiators and to avoid the gravitational pull of the enterprise to slow down or drift off focus.

To manage this nonnegotiable, changes to the Big Bet Experiment Planner should require formal discussion and approval, thus helping to maintain velocity. By using these constraints, the Big Bet team is working not just long and hard, but extremely smart and focused. The constraints work when they are real.

We know there are moments when the constraints need to be adjusted. Do so with caution and formality, such as a sign-off. Repeatedly failing to adhere to the Big Bet constraints is a key risk indicator. The team should expect hard and unpredictable work to hit deadlines. In Big Bets, this extra effort is almost a universal expectation. Ensure that this expectation is clear to the team before starting.

KEEP THINKING BIG

One of Amazon's most unique orientations is toward thinking big. Their leadership principle reads, "Thinking small is a self-fulfilling prophecy. Leaders create and communicate a bold direction that inspires results. They think differently and look around corners for ways to serve customers."[5] The *Big Bet Leadership* approach combines thinking big with testing, learning, adjusting, clarifying, and narrowing in a risk-forward manner. This helps avoid the biggest risks of betting big.

As your Big Bet progresses through the memo experiments and into prototyping and beyond, a central and value-damaging risk is allowing the "Big" in "Big Bets" to become smaller and smaller. In an orientation to manage risk or some other compromise-oriented mindset, our ambition and potential for the concept is downscaled and reduced.

This is caused by several factors, including *cognitive tunneling*. We all suffer from it. This is the technical term for becoming task-oriented. While being task-oriented is a fantastic attribute 90 percent of the time, it can lead to blindness. Blindness to impending risks, such as hurtling toward a cliff. Or the blindness that often happens with Big Bets: we get so caught up in the motion of testing our risks that we lose track of the business prize we believe this should lead to.

And as our Big Bet team becomes task oriented, they might lose sight of the "Big" in "Big Bet." The independent advisor and overseeing executive to which the DRI reports must help avoid this. How? The weekly status report and associated meeting should have exactly two predefined items on it:

First, using the Big Bet Experiment Planner, discuss status and next steps for the test results.

Second, it should include blockers or decisions to be made. Always have your Big Bet Memo Experiments in front of you and start the meeting with a brief read of the superpower statement.

This constrained agenda does several things. It does not allow the team to focus on process. It forces the team to stay focused on the outcomes and blockers to the outcome. Effort is not outcomes. Process is not progress. Only validation of outcomes is progress. What's more, it lifts everyone out of the details at least once a week to train their attention to the valuable outcome that is the ultimate goal.

Additionally, put a different meeting on the calendar separate from any additional status or progress meeting. Call this the "Think Big meeting for the Big Bet." This meeting takes an outside-in approach and asks several questions:

First, is this Big Bet still the right concept to chase, and do we believe in the underlying financial model and assumptions? Is the juice worth the squeeze?

Second, is there any idea that would potentially increase the size of the prize? Is there even more juice for the squeeze? By asking for even bigger thinking, myopia is avoided.

Here's how this might look:

Imagine an enterprise is placing a Big Bet—and that concept is to undertake a supply chain system replacement. It would allow the business to reduce manufacturing lead times from six months to one month. That would be an undeniable superpower. Certainly, a high-risk, high-reward, wicked problem.

The team has completed the Big Bet Memo Experiments and is testing the five core value drivers with large risks. During testing, there is a concern that the target transportation cost driver cannot be met. By increasing the target from a one-month to a two-month future target lead time, the team is confident that the financial driver risk can be mitigated. This seems like a smart trade-off, and the team is considering adopting two months as the adjusted superpower. Smart decision.

Maybe.

In the Think Big meeting, when asked if there are any ideas that could increase the value of this supply chain Big Bet, an outside advisor poses three questions:

1. What if you made your supply chain a marketable service to other noncompetitive companies, a supply-chain-as-a-service add-on business?

2. What would have to be true to get a negotiated transportation cost to support our one-month target?

3. What is the theoretical limit for the shortest manufacturing lead time?

These three questions jolt the Big Bet team to see future-horizon business opportunities, giving the executives and team the confidence to maintain the one-month superpower goal, as well as a few key design features for the scaling phase to consider.

MANAGE BY PROOF POINTS

Most initiatives are governed through their status reports, risk reporting, and budget reviews. This is, by nature, rolled-up and highly filtered information, making it susceptible to further filtering.

A gemba walk is a technique from lean manufacturing and kaizen management designed to give visibility to waste, quality, or production issues by putting eyes on the actual work. "Gemba" is Japanese for "actual place." A gemba walk is a method used to ask informed questions and learn about what is taking place on the factory floor. The gemba walk is like management by wandering or walking around, but differs in one critical manner: the gemba walk has a specific purpose—to identify waste and quality issues.

Because of the criticality and speed at which Big Bet initiatives need to be pursued, executives must get out of their ivory towers, walk the figurative factory floor of their business, and gain an additional boots-on-the-ground level of insight. They need to go for a gemba walk.

The best business leaders have a keen sense for Big Bet execution risk and disconnects. They take early action on that sense and use a wide range of tools and techniques to pressure test Big Bet initiatives. They keep a high sense of focus and urgency through this activity. They create an atmosphere of frank communication and give visibility to senior management to everyone who works on the team (this is one of the perks of working on Big Bets).

The successful change agent systematically and continually probes in a myriad of manners. This is pressure testing—pushing, testing, confirming, and sensing to make sure nothing starts leaking under pressure.

Through this pressure testing, leaders set a tone of "management by walking around," not relying on just reports and proxies. When facts on the ground don't match the reports, they trust the ground facts and use this truth to strengthen the reporting system.

But since our teams are, most likely, not building a physical product on a factory floor, what is our version of the gemba walk? We do this with an emphasis on proof points versus traditional activity reporting.

Add to status reporting by doing more demos, prototypes, beta testing, and early scaling tests and by employing any other opportunity to see and demonstrate progress rather than reporting on the progress. Confirm using firsthand verification by finding ways to design and schedule more proof points. Yes, do less status reporting; do more proof points and demos. In some circumstances, such as when the team is all working physically together, do away completely with weekly status reports and just produce a monthly progress report.

Above all else, orient the performance management system to the actual work of the team—demos, hypothesis testing, learning memos, and decisions. In our experience, the best senior executives are skilled at receiving the pre-meeting memo and material, digesting it, and adding comments and questions back to the team. By the time the meeting happens, everyone is discussing the implications of the material, the true strategic value, and decisions, rather than sitting there being briefed or brought up to speed. Although Amazon advocates for reading the memos in the meeting, we believe, after having implemented this memo-driven experimentation in many organizations, that the better approach is in this pre-read and comment process. But that does require the senior executives to prepare for meetings.

This can work for any reading material—key use cases, memos, anything written. You're asking someone to read the memo, not sit and have it presented. The reader can then save questions for the status meetings or Think Big meetings.

In addition to the meeting efficiency, the level of thinking is typically superior because the reader is not reacting to new material. They have been thinking about it, consciously and subconsciously, for at least a day.

Demos don't have to be an operating application, but developing a user interface and user stories in tools like Figma is almost as lightweight as doing hand-drawn prototypes. Doing the demo in rapid user interface (UI) design tools hones everyone's eye to usability and value propositions. If the demo is testing a critical risk such as a scaling risk or technical risk, design it to show the element running, under load, as well as the demonstrated test result, perhaps speed of processing and effective throughput. This isolated key-risk demo-driven orientation benefits the work priority of the team, creates urgency throughout, and shares the decision-making.

We knew one senior leader who ran "Demo Fridays," in the office when feasible, to create an orientation to short-term progress points. Key executives outside the Big Bet team were pressed to participate. This is the equivalent of "management by walking around." A monthly or quarterly Big Bet review cycle is not nearly enough involvement to truly help the team and the Big Bet.

There is one key rule or constraint that is especially important in your proof points: You must be smart about the questions you ask. Leverage the memos, approaches, and constraints written and designed in the Big Bet Thinking phase. The senior executive and anyone else participating in an active initiative performance management role must grok—deeply understand—the superpower concepts, testing approaches, and process at work.

As you manage by walking around and see the demos and proof points, understand both the value you can add and also the damage you can do. Be the chief repeating officer and not the chief diluting officer who uses inaccurate and confusing descriptions. For example, Jeff Bezos, instead of asking the merchants launch team "How's it going?" would ask "Can a merchant register and sell in the middle of the night without talking to anyone?" He grokked the superpower concept of the marketplace strategy and asked the specific right question, based on the customer superpower, to answer.

Ask the right question at the right time, not the right question at the wrong time. Because the team is testing, refining, and learning about the biggest risks early and not pursuing everything at once, questions must have the right context. The classic example of this misstep is an executive asking, "What's your revenue forecast for next year?" when the concept is still in its early stages. That question risks sending team members to spend time developing the revenue forecast when that is complete fool's gold and out of sequence. When the team is developing the scaling plan, or certainly at post-scale, that same question is a great question. Too early, it might create a risk in the initiative.

CREATE SEPARATION

Separation or segregation of duties is always at the heart of good risk management. Whether it ranges from a key internal control measure, such as separating key responsibilities or ensuring multiple signatures on key decisions, to having external directors on the board, separation and independence is always at the heart of risk management. Why are we talking about this?

There is the inherent nature of risk being actively managed throughout the Big Bet. But the silent risk is the enthusiasm and pride of ownership that develops throughout the journey of the Big Bet. This optimism is needed and overall is something required to push through the challenging work, setbacks, and frustrations. But optimism creates its own perverse set of risks to be managed. The first principle of all these approaches is independence by creating separation. Create an approach or mechanism bringing active skepticism and fresh eyes to see into and beyond the work being done on the Big Bet.

There are several ways to create separation and independence.

Assign a Red Team

A Red Team is an assigned devil's advocate. The Red Team's job is to ask hard questions, challenge plans and assumptions, and generally, take an adversarial approach to information coming from the Big Bet team.

Have you ever had someone in a meeting who just won't let it go? Just keeps coming up with tough questions, just keeps pushing for more proof, greater clarity, and deeper understanding? That person is not a pain in the ass. That person is the prototype for your Red Team. The pushier the better.

The purpose of a Red Team is not to raise your blood pressure, but to guard against cognitive biases such as groupthink and confirmation bias. When you create or retain a Red Team, the contrarian view is embraced. This is the outsider perspective that may notice the flaws—or opportunities—that the team has overlooked.

It's not a new concept. The US Army uses it. It may even have roots that stretch back to the 1500s and the reign of Pope Sixtus V, who is said to have created a "devil's advocate" position to generate robust debate around beatification.[6]

Conduct Rude Q&A

What can you do when you're a large team within an even bigger enterprise and you need to have harder conversations? We suggest the Rude Q&A.

Create a small team external to the Big Bet. This might be functional stakeholders that will be impacted by the Big Bet. Give them thorough briefings on the Big Bet, including reading all of the memos written along the way. This team of stakeholders outlines a set of hard questions and allows the team to read and prepare. Hold a half-day or one-day meeting. The prepared questions just set the broad outline of the grilling process. Have a moderator manage the dialog. Ensure that the spirit of the exercise is well understood: to ask the hard questions the team is not thinking about and to help surface risks and opportunities that have not been noticed.

The meeting is announced as Rude Q&A to explicitly signal to everyone that the job of this exercise is to ask hard questions. Set this expectation so nobody takes the probing personally. Ask each person attending, including both the people asking the hard questions and the people there to answer those hard questions, to independently write a two-page memo on key learnings and highlights from the Rude Q&A session. Memos are due within two business days of the meeting.

Involve Independent Advisors

A Big Bet "blind spot" advisor is typically not part of the business or functional unit running the Big Bet. Often these are independent contractors or consultants, retained on a part-time basis to participate in all key performance management activities and decision-making moments. But they should not be part of the Big Bet full-time team effort.

This individual works closely with the DRI, but is hired by the board, CEO, or executive overseeing the Big Bet. Is the expense of this role a luxury? On one hand, yes. It takes not just budget but effort to help this person do the job of helping the team find blind spots.

But when it works, the results are impressive.

T-Mobile's enterprise strategy team retained John Rossman in 2018 specifically as an advisor to bring new techniques and a beginner's eye to the business, and involved him on a periodic basis to read, comment, and then push, and push hard, on the thinking of the team. (This was when the *Big Bet Leadership* authors, Kevin and John, first worked together.)

The key to making this work is making the goal of the process clear. Kevin had to make clear to the team that John's job was not to write the analysis but to critique the thinking. From that basis, people were not surprised when he gave direct feedback. The typical management consultant is not equipped or used in this manner.

FEATURE THE BAD NEWS

Finally, we'll take a look at communication style relative to Big Bet status and progress and creating a risk-forward culture through performance management.

There is a wide and diverse set of stakeholders to bring along on most Big Bet journeys. Is there a communication plan, and the messaging expertise required for your Big Bet to succeed? Is communication targeted and appropriate for different stakeholders and needs? An *authentic story* is always needed and is a key part of strategy and success. This story makes your customers, your users, and the business case the hero and explains how your Big Bet gets them to the desired future state.

This is one reason why the memo experiments, when used strategically, help frame an initiative as a story used through a Big Bet to both define the outcome and remind us of the hero and the outcomes.

Do status communications get to the heart of the matter (versus being opaque, complex, and optimistic) and in succinct language? Are the "asks" similarly clear and concise?

In thirty-five years of running and participating in hundreds of projects, John's number one rule in status communications has been and remains "feature the bad news." Don't make it hard for the reader to find the issues and recommendations. Put them first. This mindset and guideline is counter to the way the vast majority of project reports and communications are architected and led. But when you feature the bad news—put it up front and highlighted—it attacks several cognitive biases and helps the entire Big Bet collective manage, execute, and make better future decisions. The reason for doing this first is found in a quote attributed to the late US Secretary of State and four-star general Colin Powell: "Bad news isn't wine. It doesn't improve with age."

The Cognitive Biases

Several key biases are mitigated by featuring the bad news:

Strategic misrepresentation—the tendency to misstate information in the moment because you hope that distortion will further your longer-term goals for the project.

Optimism bias—the tendency to let your belief in the Big Bet's eventual success color your communication at this early stage.

Planning fallacy—the tendency to underestimate issues such as cost, timing, and risk.

Sunk cost fallacy—the tendency to recommend new spending because so much has been spent already . . . even when evidence suggests this is a bad idea.

When we feature the bad news, the entire posture of the program and leadership culture changes.

A Big Bet initiative—any digital transformation or operating model transition—is just a collection of issues and risks. Operate from that assumption. When you feature the issues, feature the risks; feature the weaknesses every Big Bet has. You can deal with them. You create a leadership culture of straight talk, humility, and execution risk mitigation.

But beware! Recognize that featuring the bad news should not come at the cost of crushing a positive or optimistic demeanor or culture. In fact, it is the combination of positivity, humility, and featuring the bad news that creates positive spirit, team morale, risk mitigation, and successful Big Bet outcomes. The combination creates bold and empowered leadership and teams—ones that are successful at overly complex missions.

The underlying point of featuring the bad news is that when issues and risks are ignored, unrealized, or hidden, and optimism becomes your default position, your Big Bet initiative, not to mention *your job*, is at the most risk.

STAY VIGILANT

If the Big Bet fails due to poor execution, or an unforeseen material risk manifests later, who will be held accountable? Implementing a tuned performance management model is not a set-and-forget exercise. It needs to evolve over time. Remember, people only respect what you inspect. Inspection is done by seeing the progress and probing, not just accepting the narrative and evaluation of the team.

CONCLUSION

"Do your job."

—BILL BELICHICK

Current success or even dominance in a market is no guarantee of sustained differentiation. You know this. You feel the competition, margin compression, customer churn, difficulty in winning new customers, and retaining top talent. The lifespan of Fortune 500 companies continues to shrink, with once-dominant organizations rapidly becoming commoditized and marginalized.

This is the "innovators dilemma"—the choice between continuing to optimize in the current market and model with a focus on short-term financial results or embracing disruptive technologies and models knowing the risks and the investment this takes, with a commitment to long-term results. You cannot do both, and there is no guarantee of success. In fact, most transformations fail. But there are exceptions.

Take IBM. Since its inception in 1911, the company has perpetually reinvented itself. From its beginnings manufacturing punch-card data processing equipment to becoming a leading pioneer in the mainframe computer industry, personal computing, and later enterprise-level software, services, and cloud computing, IBM's ability to evolve has been noteworthy. They have always invested in research, development, and innovation. However, the company now stands at the brink of yet another transformation. Will it succeed or falter this time?

Or consider Netflix. Born in 1997 as a DVD-by-mail service, it upended the established models of Blockbuster and Hollywood Video. Recognizing the untapped potential of streaming technology, Netflix reinvented itself in 2007, catalyzing a revolution in media consumption. This was one strategic pivot. Then they made another high-risk transition with major investments in original content in 2013 with the release of *House of Cards*, establishing Netflix as a powerhouse in the entertainment industry. But as it currently grapples with the limits of its model and customer demand, can it successfully transition to a new high-growth and profitability trajectory?

Walmart provides an interesting case study. A titan in retail, its slow response to Amazon's rise reveals the importance of adaptability. Considering Walmart's traditional emphasis on operational excellence and financial targets, and their difficulty in changing their store-only model, they have had to become willing to make major leadership adjustments. The CEO, Doug McMillon, says of the challenge, "I'm not naturally a risk taker. I don't gamble. I don't jump off bridges with a bungee cord. I don't. I'm not a risk taker. But this company, to be here in the next generation, has to take risks."[1]

Such examples underline that Big Bets are not only possible, but necessary for survival and crucial for winning. The challenge starts with leaders, and the willingness to adjust their own personal playbooks, belief systems, time allocation, and approaches. Most leaders we have worked with see transformation as a third-person endeavor: "These are changes the organization and others need to make." They don't see it as a first-person endeavor: "What changes do I need to make?" The change starts with, and will either succeed or fail as a result of, the executives' willingness to adapt.

Companies must execute Big Bet transformations across four critical areas—customer experience, products and services, operating models, and business models—to thrive in this dynamic landscape. Satya Nadella, CEO of Microsoft, outlines his thinking on these areas: "The first is engaging their customer base by leveraging data to improve the customer experience. Second, they must empower their own employees by enabling greater and more mobile productivity and collaboration . . . Third, they must optimize operations, automating and simplifying business processes . . . Fourth, they must transform their products, services, and business models."[2]

As we hurtle into the AI-driven Hyper-Digital Era, we foresee a landscape of greater opportunity and disruption. New, unknown enterprises will rise, while invincible brands may stumble. Even behemoths like Amazon and Google, two of the big winners of the first digital era, are facing market changes and the need for significant structural changes. Jeff Bezos himself predicted Amazon's eventual fall: "I predict one day Amazon will fail. Amazon will go bankrupt. If you look at large companies, their lifespans tend to be 30-plus years, not a hundred-plus years."[3]

We advise adopting the mindset of an "active skeptic," someone who applies meticulous scrutiny before committing to a concept. Active skeptics are optimistic about innovating, but force proof-of-concept before committing. They dedicate time and resources to test feasibility and potential business value in a systematic manner—again, and again, and again. They don't proceed on investments or programs just for public perception. They realize that often the hardest competition is within the organization and in battling their past success.

Big Bet legends, leaders who successfully navigate major transformations, consistently have three essential habits: they create clarity, maintain velocity, and prioritize risk and value. They create a Big Bet Vector enabling these habits across the organization.

The spotlight is now turned to you. What principles, strategies, and priorities will you incorporate into your unique adaptation of the *Big Bet Leadership* playbook? Are you able to solve the hardest problems and lead the transformations needed? Isn't it your job to lead successful Big Bets?

WHY MEMOS?

BIG BET MEMO EXPERIMENTS

In Part I, "Big Bet Thinking" (Chapter 1, "Thinking in Outcomes," and Chapter 2, "Play Chess, Not Checkers"), we outlined a set of memos to write and debate. We believe that for most business situations, writing is the best way to capture and summarize complex business situations and thinking. But . . . the techniques and results can also be accomplished with other techniques. We are interested in the clarity of thinking and ability to communicate it to others, regardless of how it is achieved.

Throughout, we refer to memos either by a particular name or by the encompassing term of Big Bet Memo Experiments. A memo experiment simultaneously analyzes, designs, clarifies, tests, communicates, and documents the most critical aspects of our Big Bet.

When the situations are complex, subtle and active debate and best thinking are required slide presentations do not measure up. Writing in complete and structured narratives delivers far better thinking and team communication.

Research backs up this belief, showing that the act of writing is a mind-sharpening tool. When we write, the process allows the brain to connect the dots among fragments of knowledge.[1] Writing ignites the mind in a unique way and delivers a more thoughtful and knowledgeable result. The process of writing allows you to access and leverage that knowledge efficiently. This is amplified when a team engages in the writing.

Memos greatly improve the clarity of the problem diagnosis and proposed solution and prepare the team for collaboration and the eventual executive debate. A Big Bet always requires a meshing of the best thinking across multiple leaders and is often met with pushback. Writing memos and debating memos as a team creates the defensible best ideas and allows others both to contribute and gain the benefit of the combined thinking.

Writing creates a record that aids institutional memory. Slide decks are typically reliant upon the presenter's commentary to pass it forward. They contain shorthand, sentence fragments, and images that need explanation and verbal support. The commentary is not stored with the slides. Written narratives can be reviewed, repurposed, and audited in retrospect better than presentations can be.

Finally, consider your own frame of mind—your emotional and intellectual readiness to do battle. The act of writing gives the confidence boost needed to present a plan, because you are truly better prepared. Research published in the *Journal of Consulting and Clinical Psychology* suggests that the act of writing can make you feel happier and less negative.[2]

If those reasons aren't good enough, consider the typical alternative. Professor Edward Tufte of Yale University has studied the impact of computer science and graphic design—or more specifically, slideware. His research played a key role in Amazon's adoption of the narrative techniques. The use of slides versus written text is devastating, he says, for both the audience and the idea.

The problem, he says, starts with the limited space for text on any given slide. The average slide holds about forty words. But complex ideas, such as a Big Bet, demand a lot more than forty words. That means more slides and the effort needed to create readable slides and flow between them.

As the slide decks expand, the audience is pushed to its limit. Slide presentations balloon, subjecting the audience to what Tufte calls "relentless sequentiality." Slide after slide after slide. In meeting after meeting after meeting.[3]

Presenters know this and often resort to the next aspect of slideware that Tufte finds problematic—and that's the graphics. Charts are often colorful and eye-catching, but they can be poor communicators. At best, they can be confusing or interpreted in different ways. At worst, they can bend content in a way that favors visual appeal over insights and accuracy.

Attendees won't read slides. Presenters summarize the important content. And the combination dumbs-down the entire thinking process of the organizations. Especially on complex, nuanced problems and the proposals offered to solve those problems—for Big Bets—this dumbing-down does not work.

All of these advantages combined create the final rationale. Our goal is to have high-value ideas well understood, or mitigated risks be the concepts that are funded and prioritized. But what tends to happen is that mediocre ideas with high risks are funded because they are represented by charming presenters with incredible graphics and presentations. By utilizing memos and engaging in an iterative process of writing, reading, discussing, and refining these documents, our collective thinking increases while the impact of presentation theater is diminished.

Many leading companies have adopted, at least in part, this concept of memo writing to drive clarity of thinking to define the future state in their innovation and problem-solving. Examples include Amazon, Goldman Sachs,[4] Airbnb, Atlassian, Nike, and dozens of others. There are specialized collaboration products designed for memo experiments, some of which we have inspired and for which we have contributed guidance and templates.

Amazon is, no doubt, the leader in this powerful practice. They have coined the term "Working Backwards"[5] to describe their approach—start with the future customer experience, or operational capability, and work backwards. Amazon Web Services (AWS) has engaged with hundreds of their clients in Working Backwards workshops.

In his 2017 Shareholder Letter, Amazon founder Jeff Bezos addressed Amazon's culture of high standards and his committed belief that writing instead of using PowerPoint leads to clearer thinking and better decisions. Establishing a culture like this takes practice, Bezos explains. It requires a large time investment and even a coach to properly seed and develop. He equates the development of culture to that of learning a perfect handstand.

Bezos based that analogy on a dear friend's attempts to execute the perfect handstand. The friend went so far as to hire a handstand coach. But that's when she learned the hard truth: it can take six months of daily practice to learn this skill. It's just not as easy as it looks.

How does the handstand relate to the written memo? Bezos explains: The Amazon rule against PowerPoints insists that every meeting begin with the silent reading of the meeting leader's six-page memo. Some of these memos are brilliant, Bezos said. Some, he acknowledged, "come in at the other end of the spectrum."[6]

Most leaders at Amazon could recognize a great memo. They know it when they see it, Bezos noted. But most of them couldn't articulate why it was great.

This is where the handstand story is applicable. Just as Bezos's friend was surprised and dismayed to learn that perfecting the handstand would take six months, many leaders at Amazon were surprised to learn that producing great memos takes time and practice. They can't be dashed off in few hours. They take revisions, feedback, downtime, and then more revisions. It is not a quick process.

We embrace the Bezos writing timeline—and offer our help in achieving that skill level. By adapting for the mission of Big Bets, and by helping dozens of companies utilize a memo-centric process to enhance their outcomes, we've created a Big Bet purpose-built approach to accelerate this learning curve.

The Big Bet Memos organize, rationalize, and explain the Big Bet Vector. They enable a team to develop better thinking, and enable key stakeholders to grok—to deeply understand—our position, the options available, and the decisions needed, and to contribute to the concepts. While writing and sweating the details of specific words and the cohesiveness of the logic may seem like the slow path to success, it is the fastest and cheapest type of experimentation. Writing is experimentation. Writing clear, concise memos is the superpower for establishing the Big Bet Vector.

AUTHORS' NOTE

To our Big Bet readers:

We look forward to reading the customer reviews of our book or hearing from you directly at info@rossmanpartners.com.

We eagerly anticipate hearing your stories of triumph—or failure—and sharing your path in Big Bet leadership. It is our hope that you will leverage the resources available at www.BigBetLeadership. com. Resources available to readers include behind-the-scenes videos, templates, and a growing number of examples that can be used to help accelerate your progress.

John Rossman now offers keynote addresses and workshops on the theme of Big Bet Leadership. Learn more at www.johnrossman.com.

Sincerely,
John Rossman & Kevin McCaffrey

ENDNOTES

PREFACE

1 Congressional Budget Office, Budget and Economic Data, Long-term Budget Projections, June 2023. Entitlement programs include Social Security, Medicare, Medicaid, CHIP, and Marketplace Subsidies. https://www.cbo.gov/data/budget-economic-data#1.

2 Bain & Company, Global Private Equity Report 2023, https://www.bain.com/insights/topics/global-private-equity-report/.

3 National Venture Capital Association, 2023 Yearbook, https://nvca.org/recommends/2023-yearbook/.

4 Data compiled from the companies' 10-K reports.

2012 reports:

Amazon: https://www.sec.gov/Archives/edgar/data/1018724/000119312513028520/d445434d10k.htm; Apple: https://www.sec.gov/Archives/edgar/data/320193/000119312512444068/d411355d10k.htm; Facebook: https://www.sec.gov/Archives/edgar/data/1326801/000132680113000003/fb-12312012x10k.htm; Google: https://www.sec.gov/Archives/edgar/data/1288776/000119312513028362/d452134d10k.htm; Microsoft: https://www.sec.gov/Archives/edgar/data/789019/000119312512316848/d347676d10k.htm.

2022 reports:

Amazon: https://www.sec.gov/Archives/edgar/data/1018724/000101872423000004/amzn-20221231.htm; Apple: https://www.sec.gov/Archives/edgar/data/320193/000032019322000108/aapl-20220924.htm; Facebook (Meta): https://www.sec.gov/Archives/edgar/data/1326801/000132680123000013/meta-20221231.htm; Google (Alphabet): https://www.sec.gov/Archives/edgar/data/1652044/000165204423000016/

goog-20221231.htm; Microsoft: https://www.sec.gov/Archives/edgar/data/789019/000156459022026876/msft-10k_20220630.htm.

5   Jeff Bezos, Amazon 2014 Letter to Shareholders, 2015. https://www.sec.gov/Archives/edgar/data/1018724/000119312515144741/d895323dex991.htm.

INTRODUCTION

1   Peter Bendor-Samuel, Everest Group, "Why Digital Transformations Fail: 3 Exhausting Reasons," blog posted August 27, 2019, https://www.everestgrp.com/2019-08-why-digital-transformations-fail-3-exhausting-reasons-blog-51164.html.

2   Eric Lamarre, Kate Smaje, and Rodney Zemmel, *Rewired: The McKinsey Guide to Outcompeting in the Age of Digital and AI* (New York: Wiley, 2023), p. 26, Kindle.

3   Clayton M. Christensen, Richard Alton, Curtis Rising, and Andrew Waldeck, "The Big Idea: The New M&A Playbook," March 2011, *Harvard Business Review*, https://hbr.org/2011/03/the-big-idea-the-new-ma-playbook.

4   Bent Flyvbjerg and Alexander Budzier, "Why Your IT Project May Be Riskier Than You Think," *Harvard Business Review*, September 2011, https://hbr.org/2011/09/why-your-it-project-may-be-riskier-than-you-think.

5   Bent Flyvbjerg and Dan Gardner, *How Big Things Get Done* (New York: Crown Currency, 2023), p. 8, Kindle.

6   Richard P. Rumelt, *Good Strategy/Bad Strategy: The Difference and Why it*

Matters (New York: Crown Business, 2011).

7   Suzanne Kappner, "Bed Bath & Beyond Used to Be Great. These Two Are Why," *Wall Street Journal*, January 27, 2023, https://www.wsj.com/articles/bed-bath-beyond-bankruptcy-stock-founders-11674778627

8   Chris Bradley, Martin Hirt, and Sven Smit, "Strategy to Beat the Odds," *McKinsey Quarterly*, February 13, 2018, https://www.mckinsey.com/capabilities/strategy-and-corporate-finance/our-insights/strategy-to-beat-the-odds.

9   Bradley, "Strategy."

CHAPTER 1

1   Jeff Shore, "These 10 Peter Drucker Quotes May Change Your World," NBC News, September 16, 2014, https://www.nbcnews.com/id/wbna56060818.

2   If the term "killer feature" is not smart for your product, perhaps for a car or healthcare scenario, use "lovable feature."

3   If the word "sucks" is not appropriate for your company, use "unbearable" or "agonizing." The key is to find the critical customer or problem pain.

4   Eric Ries, *The Lean Startup* (New York: Crown Business, 2011).

5   Denise Chow, "To Cheaply Go: How Falling Launch Costs Fueled a Thriving Economy in Orbit," NBC News, April 8, 2022, https://www.nbcnews.com/science/space/space-launch-costs-growing-business-industry-rcna23488.

6   Magdalena Petrova, "Why Elon

Musk's Boring Company Is Finding that Traffic Is Tough to Fix," CNBC.com, July 2, 2021, https://www.cnbc.com/2021/07/20/why-elon-musks-boring-company-is-finding-that-traffic-is-tough-to-fix.html.

7 Marcus Lu, "Charted: Tesla's Unrivaled Profit Margins," Visual Capitalist, February 3, 2003, https://www.visualcapitalist.com/charted-teslas-unrivaled-profit-margins/.

8 Tim Higgins, "Elon Musk's Cost-Cutting Targets at Tesla Pressure EV Rivals," *Wall Street Journal*, March 20, 2023, https://www.wsj.com/articles/elon-musks-cost-cutting-targets-put-pressure-on-ev-rivals-724d881b.

9 Sebastian Herrera, "Amazon Expands Same-Day Delivery, With Fees, While Battling Slow Growth," *Wall Street Journal*, February 26, 2023, https://www.wsj.com/articles/amazon-expands-same-day-delivery-with-fees-while-battling-slow-growth-344bd3a6.

10 Tai Kim, "Warren Buffet Believes This Is 'The Most Important Thing' to Find in a Business," CNBC.com, May 7, 2018, https://www.cnbc.com/2018/05/07/warren-buffett-believes-this-is-the-most-important-thing-to-find-in-a-business.html.

CHAPTER 2

1 John Schwartz, "Appreciation," July 15, 1994, https://www.washingtonpost.com/archive/lifestyle/1994/07/15/appreciation/475eb32e-b5ca-45d1-8d56-a2694c619d40/.

2 Wikipedia, "Gary Kildall," https://en.wikipedia.org/wiki/Gary_Kildall.

3 Wikipedia, "Seattle Computer Products," https://en.wikipedia.org/wiki/Seattle_Computer_Products.

4 Hannah Bae, "Bill Gates' 40th Anniversary Email: Goal Was 'A Computer On Every Desk,'" CNN Business, April 6, 2015, https://money.cnn.com/2015/04/05/technology/bill-gates-email-microsoft-40-anniversary/index.html.

5 Wikipedia, "Wintel," https://en.wikipedia.org/wiki/Wintel.

6 Ron Friedman, *Decoding Greatness: How the Best in the World Reverse Engineer Success* (New York: Simon and Schuster, 2021).

7 Steven Johnson, *Where Good Ideas Come From: The Natural History of Innovation* (New York: Riverhead, 2010).

8 Adapted from Friedman, *Decoding Greatness*, Chap. 2.

9 Wikipedia, "Bill & Melinda Gates Foundation," https://en.wikipedia.org/wiki/Bill_%26_Melinda_Gates_Foundation.

10 Bill & Melinda Gates Foundation, "About: Committed to fighting the greatest inequities," https://www.gatesfoundation.org/about.

11 John C. Camillus, "Strategy as a Wicked Problem," *Harvard Business Review*, May 2008, https://hbr.org/2008/05/strategy-as-a-wicked-problem.

12 Satya Nadella, "The Learn-It-All Does Better Than the Know-It-All," Wall Street Journal Future of Work panel, January 23, 2019, https://www.wsj.com/video/satya-nadella-the-learn-it-all-does-better-than-the-know-it-all/D8BC205C-D7F5-423E-8A41-0E921E86597C.html.

CHAPTER 3

1   Adam Lashinsky, "How Apple Works: Inside the World's Biggest Startup," Fortune Classic, May 9, 2011, https://docplayer.net/205254025-How-apple-works-inside-the-world-s-biggest-startup.html.

2   Lashinsky, "How Apple Works."

3   Jeff Dyer and Hal Gregersen, "How Does Amazon Stay At Day One?" Forbes, August 8, 2017, https://www.forbes.com/sites/innovatorsdna/2017/08/08/how-does-amazon-stay-at-day-one/?sh=f5b5d357e4d

4   Dyer, "How Does Amazon?"

5   Palantir Technologies Inc., "Palantir and Panasonic Energy of North America Sign Multi-year Agreement," June 7, 2023, https://investors.palantir.com/news-details/2023/Palantir-and-Panasonic-Energy-of-North-America-sign-multi-year-agreement/.

6   Cynthia Littleton, "10 Takeaways From Bob Iger's 'The Ride of a Lifetime': Big Deals, 'Love, Sinatra' and His Best Hire," Variety, October 4, 2019, https://variety.com/2019/biz/news/bob-iger-book-disney-ride-of-a-lifetime-1203358715/.

7   Attributed to Paul Graham. This quote appears with slightly different wording at https://www.ycombinator.com/library/4D-yc-s-essential-startup-advice and https://medium.com/panacea/how-to-avoid-startup-suicide-toxic-founder-relationships-a8a0d746a82b.

8   Jessica Stillman, "This Ex-Googler's Scathing Takedown of the Company Is Basically a Blueprint for Killing Innovation," Inc., February 28, 2023, https://www.inc.com/jessica-stillman/this-ex-googler-scathing-takedown-of-the-company-is-basically-a-blueprint-for-killing-innovation.html.

CHAPTER 4

1   Henry Blodget, "I Asked Jeff Bezos the Tough Questions—No Profits, the Book Controversies, the Phone Flop—And He Showed Why Amazon Is Such a Huge Success," Insider, December 16, 2014, https://www.businessinsider.com/amazons-jeff-bezos-the-business-insider-interview-2014-12.

2   Blodget, "I Asked Jeff Bezos."

3   John Cook, "Jeff Bezos on Innovation: Amazon 'Willing to Be Misunderstood for Long Periods of Time,'" GeekWire, June 7, 2011, https://www.geekwire.com/2011/amazons-bezos-innovation/.

4   Jeff Bezos, Amazon 2014 Letter to Shareholders, 2015. https://www.sec.gov/Archives/edgar/data/1018724/000119312515144741/d895323dex991.htm.

5   David J. Bland and Alexander Osterwalder, Testing Business Ideas: A Field Guide for Rapid Experimentation (Hoboken, NJ: Wiley, 2020), https://www.strategyzer.com/books/testing-business-ideas-david-j-bland.

CHAPTER 5

1   Monica Bulger, Patrick McCormick, and Mikaela Pitcan, "The Legacy of inBloom," Data & Society, February 2, 2017, https://datasociety.net/pubs/ecl/InBloom_feb_2017.pdf.

2   Adam Grant, *Originals: How Nonconformists Move the World* (New York: Penguin, 2016), p. 75, Kindle.

3   All quotes in this paragraph are from Grant, Originals, pp. 75 and 76, Kindle.

4   Chip Heath and Dan Heath, *Switch: How to Change When Change Is Hard* (New York: Crown Business, 2010).

5   Adapted from Heath, *Switch*.

6   Alexandra Gibbs, "Microsoft CEO Satya Nadella on the 3 Qualities that Make a Great Leader," CNBC.com, https://www.cnbc.com/2019/02/26/mwc-microsoft-satya-nadella-on-leadership-qualities.html.

7   Wikipedia, "Backcasting," https://en.wikipedia.org/wiki/Backcasting.

8   Andy Jassy, "2021 Letter to Shareholders," Amazon, https://www.aboutamazon.com/news/company-news/2021-letter-to-shareholders.

9   Ayse Birsel, "Why Elon Musk Spends 80 Percent of His Time on This 1 Activity," Inc., July 21, 2017, https://www.inc.com/ayse-birsel/why-elon-musk-spends-80-percent-of-his-time-on-thi.html.

10   Lawrence Kasdan and Leigh Brackett, The Empire Strikes Back, Internet Movie Script Database, https://imsdb.com/scripts/Star-Wars-The-Empire-Strikes-Back.html.

CHAPTER 6

1   "Netflix Shares Sink Again as Analysts Dig into Qwikster," *Hollywood Reporter*, September 20, 2011, https://www.yahoo.com/entertainment/s/netflix-shares-sink-again-analysts-dig-qwikster-175003276.html.

2   GE Digital webcast presentation, June 23, 2016, https://www.ge.com/sites/default/files/ge_webcast_presentation_06232016_1.pdf.

3   Steve Lohr, "Preaching from the Ballmer Pulpit," *New York Times*, January 28, 2007, https://www.nytimes.com/2007/01/28/business/yourmoney/28ballmer.html.

4   "How Amazon Prime's Subscription Management Service Was Invented," interview with Neil Roseman and Jorrit Van der Meulen, Invent like an Owner with Dave Schappell podcast, minute 30, https://podcasts.apple.com/us/podcast/invent-like-an-owner-with-dave-schappell/id1561085173?i=1000527339587.

CHAPTER 7

1   Note: In our view, overt misalignment is much less insidious and can even be highly productive if addressed through healthy decision-making processes (discussed in Chapter 6). It's the unspoken, quiet, hidden misalignment that is particularly dangerous.

2   Kat Eschner, "The Story of the Real Canary in the Coal Mine," *Smithsonian Magazine*, December 30, 2016, https://www.smithsonianmag.com/smart-news/story-real-canary-coal-mine-180961570/.

3   Ralph Bodin, Thomas J. Chermack, and Laura M. Coons, "The Effects of Scenario Planning on Participant Decision-Making Style: A Quasi-Experimental Study of Four Companies," *Journal of Future Studies*, June

2016, https://jfsdigital.org/2016-2/ vol-20-no-4-june-2016/article/the-effects-of-scenario-planning-on-participant-decision-making-style-a-quasi-experimental-study-of-four-companies/; PDF found at https://doi.org/10.6531/JFS.2016.20(4).A21.

4   J. Peter Scoblic, "Learning from the Future," *Harvard Business Review*, July-August 2020, https://hbr.org/2020/07/learning-from-the-future#learning-from-the-future.

CHAPTER 8

1   That's right—Bossman Rossman. Meet Bossman at www.rossmanpartners.com/bossman.

2   McKinsey Company, "Why do most transformations fail? A conversation with Harry Robinson," Perspectives on Transformation, July 10, 2019, https://www.mckinsey.com/capabilities/transformation/our-insights/perspectives-on-transformation.

3   Wikipedia, "Tractor beam," https://en.wikipedia.org/wiki/Tractor_beam.

4   Economic Club of Washington, The David Rubenstein Show, September 13, 2018, https://www.youtube.com/watch?v=zN1PyNwjHpc.

5   Amazon, "Leadership Principles," https://www.amazon.jobs/content/en/our-workplace/leadership-principles.

6   Tim Brinkhof, "Devil's Advocate Used to Be an Actual Job within the Catholic Church," Big Think, July 11, 2022, https://bigthink.com/high-culture/devil-advocate-catholic-church/.

CONCLUSION

1   Jason Del Rey, *Winner Sells All: Amazon, Walmart and the Battle for Our Wallets, read by Roger Wayne* (New York: HarperAudio, 2023), Audible audio ed., Chap. 17, ~52-minute mark.

2   Satya Nadella, Greg Shaw, and Jill Tracie Nichols, *Hit Refresh: The Quest to Rediscover Microsoft's Soul and Imagine a Better Future for Everyone* (New York: Harper Business, 2017), p. 126.

3   Eugene Kim, "Jeff Bezos to Employees: 'One Day, Amazon Will Fail' but Our Job Is to Delay It as Long as Possible," CNBC, November 15, 2018, https://www.cnbc.com/2018/11/15/bezos-tells-employees-one-day-amazon-will-fail-and-to-stay-hungry.html.

APPENDIX

1   National Commission on Writing in America's Schools and Colleges, "The Neglected 'R': The Need for a Writing Revolution," April 2003, https://archive.nwp.org/cs/public/print/resource/2523.

2   James W. Pennebaker, Janice K. Kiecolt-Glaser, and Ronald Glaser, "Disclosure of Traumas and Immune Function: Health Implications for Psychotherapy," *Journal of Consulting and Clinical Psychology* 56 (1988), 239–245.

3   Edward Tufte, "PowerPoint Is Evil." *Wired*, September 1, 2003, https://www.wired.com/2003/09/ppt2/.

4   Dakin Campbell, "A New Goldman Sachs Tech Exec Hired from Amazon Is Taking a Page from the Jeff Bezos Playbook by Urging Engineers to Ditch PowerPoint and Write Memos," *Insider*, November 15, 2019,